PIMPOLOGY

THE 48 LAWS OF THE GAME

PIMPIN' KEN
WITH KAREN HUNTER

SIMON SPOTLIGHT ENTERTAINMENT

NEW YORK • LONDON • TORONTO • SYDNEY • NEW DELHI

NOTE TO READERS: THE NAMES OF
CERTAIN INDIVIDUALS DISCUSSED
IN THIS BOOK HAVE BEEN CHANGED.

SIMON SPOTLIGHT ENTERTAINMENT
A Division of Simon & Schuster
1230 Avenue of the Americas
New York, New York 10020

Copyright © 2007 by Ken Ivy

All insert photos are courtesy of the author's personal collection.

First Simon Spotlight Entertainment trade paperback edition August 2008

SIMON SPOTLIGHT ENTERTAINMENT and colophon are trademarks of
Simon & Schuster, Inc.

For Information about special discounts for bulk purchases, please contact
Simon & Schuster special Sales at 1-800-456-6798 or
business@simonandschuster.com

Manufactured in the United States of America

20 19 18 17 16 15

Library of Congress Cataloging-in-Publication Data

Pimpin' Ken.
Pimpology : the 48 laws of the game /
by Pimpin' Ken with Karen Hunter.
p. cm.
ISBN 978-1-4169-3844-6
ISBN 978-1-4169-6104-8 (pbk)
1. Pimps. 2. Life skills—Handbooks, manuals, etc.
I. Hunter, Karen. II. Title.
HQ115.P56 2007
646.70086'92—dc22   2007016419

P
I
M
P
O
L
O
G
Y

For my father,
Collie Ivy (a.k.a. Johnny Slick)

CONTENTS

INTRODUCTION

Pimps Are Born, Not Sworn

There are only two categories of people: pimps and hoes. You either give orders or you take them. You are either the kind of person who will have people working for you, bringing you the money, or you are the kind of person who will work for someone else, hand over your hard-earned dough, and let someone tell you what to do. That's all pimpin' is—control, mastering another. This reality may be offensive to some, but it's real, and if you open your eyes to what is truly going on in this world, you will see that everyone falls into one category or the other.

The absolute best pimps—business tycoons, power brokers, and politicians—don't have girls on the streets working the tracks, but they do make countless dollars living off of other people's intelligence and hard work. Good pimps don't have to steal or take anyone's money by force, because hoes will *give* pimps their money willingly. When you go downtown and see an old lady feeding a bird, the bird comes every day to check the lady for that bread, and the old lady chooses to come every day to be down with the bird—even that bird is pimpin'!

The biggest, baddest, most powerful pimp of all time is named Uncle Sam. Every April fifteenth he tells you to "Break yourself, bitch!" Uncle Sam can reach into your pocket at any time and take what he wants, and if you try to stop him, he puts your ass under pimp arrest. Instead of the man in the red, white, and blue suit with the top hat, they need to dress Uncle Sam in a fly Versace suit, some gators, and a jewel-encrusted cane!

I was born a pimp. My daddy was a hustler, and I learned about pimpin' from him—both the good and the bad. He was a womanizer, a pool shark, and he shot dice. He was my first role model. His actions showed me how to manipulate people. My daddy didn't have any respect for a ho, and no ho could tell my daddy what to do. He treated hoes like shit, but they still kept coming around him anyway. He used to whip their asses, beat them, send them to the hospital, and still they never left. This taught me that there was a power men could have over others, making them do anything and take anything thrown at them.

I didn't follow exactly in my father's footsteps. I created my own pathway right beside his. Instead of using terror and violence, I developed my own form of persuasion. I use psychological warfare, or pimpology, to get what I want, which is often more treacherous than physical abuse. I use words and gestures to get others to act right and do right.

The aim of this book is not to teach people how to pimp, but to promote the pimp mentality. If you don't have it, then you're apt to be somebody's ho. I have been a life-long student of this game, and I developed my own style, my own way of getting what I wanted—not just from a ho, but from *any* situation.

LAW 1

Purse First, Ass Last

If a pimp is going to take a chance, a bitch must give him money in advance. —Father Divine

THE LIFE

A pimp associate of mine, Little Bear, came from a distinguished line of pimps. His daddy was one of the biggest pimps in Milwaukee when I was growing up. Pimpin' was in Little Bear, not on him. Years ago, Little Bear was running an after-hours joint. Many pimps had these little clubs back in the day as a way of catching hoes. A bunch of us were in his joint when one of the finest hoes I ever saw walked in. She had a body like an hourglass. She was so fine her mama should have had triplets. She was just a gorgeous ho. The scene was live, but when this ho walked in, the place stopped.

Sammy, a half-ass pimp who was sitting in the corner blurted out, "That bitch so fine, she don't need no choosing fee to fuck with my pimpin'!"

Out of nowhere Little Bear jumped up and said, "Bitch, break yourself!"

She walks up to Little Bear and asks, "Mr. Bear, what

can you do with this money that I can't do with it myself? If you can answer that, I will break myself."

"Bitch, I'm the pimp and you're the ho," he said. "So act like the quarterback and pass the motherfucking bankroll."

She smiled and gave him the trap money. Little Bear then turned to me. "That's a fine-ass bitch," he said. "As soon as she makes me twenty Gs, I'm going to have some buck-naked fun with her." Then he posed the same question he'd been asked to me. "Pimpin', what could *you* do with that money?"

I stood up, because I was about to perform, and I wanted everyone to hear. "For the record," I started, "I mean to say, for the album—because the record is too short—if any of you suckers want to know what a pimp can do with that money that a bitch can't, go to the motherfucking hardware store, get you some duct tape, tape that money on the wall, and piss on it. That's what a pimp can do that a bitch can't!"

The Ism

"Purse first, ass last" is the motto of pimpin', the very foundation on which pimpin' is built. What separates a pimp from a trick is that a pimp completely flips the game. A trick pays a ho for the pussy, but a ho doesn't get to fuck a pimp until *she pays him*. A ho has got to put it in a pimp's pocket like a rocket before pimpin' can begin. It's not about a pimp breaking a ho, it's about a ho breaking herself. Violating this first law will guarantee a pimp a career of troubles and stress. If a woman can try you before she buy you, then, as B.B. King says, "The thrill is gone."

In life what is expensive seems valuable, and what's available for free seems worthless. You've heard that no one buys the cow when the milk is free, but what they didn't tell you is that after a while, no one even wants that free milk. To be valued, the key is not to give, but to receive—the more, the better. You don't want to "earn" your price, you want to "cost" it. This is the psychology behind the whole game: anything worth having, you must pay for up front.

LAW 2

Get a Name in a Game

A good name is like a credit card, you can use it when you don't have no cash at all. —Dope Man

THE LIFE

My daddy's name was Collie, but people called him Johnny Slick, because he was always hustling somebody. If he wasn't beating people in pool, he was cheating them in dice. Johnny Slick was known in the pool halls up and down Madison Avenue and Sixty-third Street in Chicago. He was also known on the streets, because he couldn't lose at shooting craps. He built his name himself, and he taught me the power of public relations and how to build a reputation.

"Nigga, I'm Johnny Slick!" he would yell in the streets. "Can't nobody fuck with me! I'm the greatest!" After hearing it often enough, people were convinced.

As far back as I can remember, my daddy used to sit my four brothers and me down and make us say his name. "Who am I?"

"Johnny Slick!" we'd all have to say in unison.

"What's my name, boys?"

"Johnny Slick!"

We would go through this shit for hours sometimes, and I would be so mad. But once I hit the streets and saw how many niggas respected my pops, it dawned on me that he was trying to teach us the importance of having a name. I used to go places and ask people if they knew my father, and they always did.

When I was around fifteen years old, I used to hang hard with my man JD a.k.a. Father Divine, who was also fifteen. Neither one of us had a driver's license, but we had lots of money from hustling. On the weekends we would rent a nice, shiny stretch limo and drive through our neighborhood, hanging out of the sunroof, throwing stacks of dollars onto the street. With each handful we would shout our names. People would be going crazy. I would throw out about three hundred singles, and with each handful I would say, "This is from Ken Ivy, y'all!"

We started dressing like the pimps, shopping where they shopped, like Nile Bush and Brass Loop. We would go to school dressed like that. Our teachers looked at us like we had lost our minds, but the kids loved us. Everybody wanted to kick it with us, and all of the older girls wanted to take us to the school dances. We were so popular that we never had to pay to get into those dances. We had already made the investment.

By the time he turned sixteen, JD was an official

pimp, with three certified hoes. He was popping like a motherfucker with his pimpin'. His name was ringing like a cell phone. I watched how much shine he was getting, and I wanted some too. One day we were at his house—him, his three hoes, and me. We were sitting at the table, just kicking it, and I said, "Man, I got to get into this pimp shit."

"No problem," JD said. "I got three hoes. Which one do you want?"

"The light-skinned one," I said, not believing he was going to give me my pick. Her name was Red.

"Bitch, excuse my pimpin'," he said. "But you're with my little brother now."

I don't know who was happier, the ho or me. She was smiling like Miss Kool-Aid. "JD, here's what we're going to do," I told him. I was always cooking up a plan. "We're going to hang out with the older pimps and steal their game right from under them."

"Lil' bro, all we need to do is what I'm already doing— look good, smell good, and keep a fresh Fleetwood," he said. He was telling me to just build my name and the rest would come—hoes, respect, money, and power. If people respect you, you got it made.

I was able to quickly get a name in my own backyard, but the real test came when I decided to broaden my pimpin'. I decided to go to the biggest city in America— New York—and see how good my pimpin' was. I got to

New York, and the stakes got higher. The pimps up there were so big, I had to really get it right. I couldn't have been in town more than two hours before I got knocked for the ho I brought with me. My first day in New York, and I got peeled. I was up there by myself, so I had to devise a plan not only to make sure I had me a ho to pimp, but also to get me a big name in the Big Apple. I had to get creative, and quick. I was pimpin' like crazy, and I decided that every time I peeled a pimp for his ho, I would give him a *Wall Street Journal* folded around a banana.

"It's in the news, you just been peeled!" I would tell him.

If the nigga wanted to talk some shit, I would put a bottle of ketchup under his tire and tell him, "You better catch up, because my game is as thick as Heinz, and yours will never be as thick as mine!" This would really make a pimp mad. Once I had him mad, he would be talking. The more he talked, the more he spread my name, and the more respect I started getting on the street. People were impressed with my style of serving a nigga. Nobody was doing the things that I was doing.

As I was trying to knock those hoes, I would drive around the track, throwing Payday candy bars out my window. "Make it a Pimpin' Ken payday, bitch!" I would say, trying to hit a ho on her ass with the candy bar.

"Who is that nigga who keeps harassing us with candy bars?" the hoes wanted to know, and they soon found out. Pimps wanted to talk to me about my tactics, because it was really pissing them off. When a pimp confronted me, I was prepared. I would make sure to always have a bunch of lollipops handy and would give one to the angry pimp.

"What's this for?" he would ask.

"It's for you, sucker!" I was always looking for a witty saying or looking to give some sort of speech, because I knew that would stick with people. Sometimes I could see it in a pimp's eyes that he wanted to kill my ass, but pimpin' is a noncontact sport. This is the NPA—the National Pimpin' Association—and I was number 23. I was the motherfucking Mack-a-Jordan of that shit.

Once I conquered New York City, I needed to take my name to the next level. I moved to Atlanta and decided to make a name for myself in hip-hop. I went to the clubs where the rappers hung out, shook hands with everybody in the club, and started talking to everyone there. After I was known, rappers started coming up to me. Once I had the ATL love, my next move was to get in their videos, talk on their albums, and get invited to all of the parties. I told them, "Y'all fuck with me and my name on the streets, and that gives you street credibility. If I fuck with y'all, then I get that rap and hip-hop credibility." I ended up on stage with OutKast at the BET Awards, and I was featured on Jermaine Dupri's album. Ultimately, it was them, Lil' Flip, 50, T.I., Nelly, and Lil Jon who made my name internationally known.

THE ISM

When you first come in the game, nobody pays you any attention. You got to keep your name popping, until others keep it popping for you. It's not about being liked or loved, it's about being respected. When people hear your name, they have to first know who you are, then they must know that you are good at what you do. A name is nothing unless people can associate it with something extraordinary. You have to have something to back it—some unique talent or knowledge. First make sure you have something to offer, or else you will be building a name in vain. Like my daddy used to say, "You got to make sure they know you *and* respect you!"

LAW 3

Don't Chase 'Em, Replace 'Em

Give that bitch a Chinese name:
Long Gone! —Pimpin' Poke

THE LIFE

The first girl I ever liked was named Candy, and she was
the finest girl in the eighth grade. I was the flyest dude in
the eighth grade, so it was only natural that the two of us
got together. I was thirteen and had very little knowledge
about the game, so I was on some square shit, such as
falling in love. I'd had other girls, but I thought Candy
was the *one*. Then one of my partners at the time let me
know that this older cat in the hood was poking Candy. I
tried to get her back, but the more I chased her, the more
she ran. When I got tired of chasing her, I got smart. I
said, "Fuck her!" and ended up going after the girl Candy
hated the most, her worst enemy. Of course, she didn't
like that, and she wanted to get back with me. I ignored
her, though.

That experience prepared me well for the shit that
would go down in the game. When a ho left me, I would

throw a party. I thought about all of the fun I had with the ho's bread, and I knew that she was only making room for the next ho with some dough. I learned a long time ago that hoes belong to the community. They look better going than they do coming, and they can "git on like they been shit on." At the height of my career I was knocking hoes back-to-back. They were coming in and going out regularly. Every time a ho got out on me, another one was bumping into her on the way in. One day my bottom bitch said, "Daddy, you don't care about us, do you?"

I said, "I like who likes me, but a ho comes to pay and be on her way. I don't need 'em, I let the Welfare feed 'em."

When I first came home from the joint, my man Father Divine had three hoes in his Jaguar. Three weeks later, he pulled up with four hoes—and three of them were new. *Damn*, I thought, *hoes change man like money changes hands*.

About fifteen years ago one of my partners, Flip (rest in peace), was just getting his feet wet, but he was sharp in the game. When we were pimpin' in Milwaukee, his name was something different. When he moved to D.C., he changed it. As we were riding down Georgia Avenue, I asked him, "Pimpin', I've been knowing you for a long time, why'd you change your name to Flip?"

"Man, I've been out here for a year," he said of his time in D.C. "And I done flipped about fifty bitches, knocking these niggas' socks off. Man, these hoes are not dedicated at all! They will fuck with me. The next day they're fucking with Smiley. Then they leave him and start fucking with Shorty P. Then Grit come and knocks all of those bitches. I got to just break them and keep it moving. I don't get emotional with none of these hoes. I don't chase them, I just pimp on the next ho."

"I dig that," I said. "If a bitch will leave her mama, she will definitely leave a pimp. Mother had 'em, mother fuck 'em."

The Ism

If you're not laced and you try pimpin' with your heart, you will lose before you even start. In any situation the one doing the chasing is more apt to be played out. If someone knows they are being chased, they are in the driver's seat, and they will usually take advantage. The one who can control his emotions will be the one to control the relationship or situation. Never put yourself at the mercy of someone else—always be mentally prepared to have a replacement step in, if need be.

LAW 4

Keep a Ho in Arrears

A bitch of mine better not keep a dime.
—Kenny Red

THE LIFE

I had this ho from Chicago. She was always asking me why she couldn't have any money. "A bitch gets no dough," I told her. "And that's how pimpin' goes."

"Naw, that's not why," she said.

"Okay, Einstein ho, why?"

"Because as long as you have all the money, I can never pay the bills. I can never buy my own clothes. I can never eat unless you say so," she said. "You do this to control my actions and keep me totally dependent on you. Plus, I can't think for myself. And if I try to leave, I will leave with nothing—basically the clothes on my back. So basically, I will always need you."

I stopped her right there. "Yeah, but bitch, I have to listen to all of your problems," I told her. "I have to teach you how to make the money you say you can't keep. And if you go to jail, I have to take the money you say you can't keep and bail you out. This is your choice. I'm sure in the course of the day, you run into four police cars, two ambulances, and a dogcatcher. You don't ask one person to save you from pimpin'. As I see it, you *like* to depend on me."

THE ISM

A pimp says he keeps a ho in the hole because she is irresponsible. But the real reason is that the more someone depends on you, the more power you have over them. To master someone completely, they have to depend on you for everything. When a pimp first gets with a ho, he tells her to break herself—after that she will only see money long enough to bring it to him.

Because he can only manage the money she makes, a pimp depends on a ho at least as much as she depends on him. But the key for a pimp is to make that ho think that she always needs him. He talks a good game, seems wise and knowledgeable, and she wants to believe she needs him to handle things. The better you talk, the more people depend on you. Since hoes like to feel taken care of, they agree to let pimps handle everything—even if they know deep down that they *could* have the upper hand. Not wanting to take it is what makes someone a ho in the first place.

LAW 5

Prey on the Weak

A bitch's weakness is a pimp's sweetness.
—Pimpin' Ken

THE LIFE

It usually starts with tears. I will see a ho crying for seemingly no reason at all, and I seize the moment. "Say, bitch. What's the matter?" I ask in my most concerned voice.

"Nothing," she sniffles.

"Oh, you know you can tell Daddy *anything*," I say.

The story eventually comes out. It usually is a similar story: "I was raped as a little girl," or "I was abused and I feel real bad about myself."

"If I see that motherfucker, I will kill him," I say to her. "But how can you feel bad about yourself? You are making two hundred, three hundred dollars an hour. You can make more than a thousand dollars a day. You have men telling you how beautiful you are. Some of these tricks are saying that they want to marry you. You may have started off in the ghetto, living in some shit hole, but you're going to end up with furs, diamonds, and even a home."

I knew this one ho, Prissy, who didn't look at all like she belonged. I asked her, "Damn, bitch. Why are you out here doing this?"

"I can't stand those motherfuckers," she said, speaking about her parents. "I want to be my own person."

"Say, bitch, imagine their faces if they saw you fucking with me. Success is the best revenge, right?"

THE ISM

Most hoes have low self-esteem for a reason. A pimp looks for that weakness, and if it isn't on the surface, he brings that motherfucker out of them. It doesn't matter to a pimp what hoes' weaknesses are, so long as they have them. Then he uses those weaknesses to his advantage.

Weakness is the best trait a person can find in someone they want to control. If you can't find a weakness, you have to create one. You have to tear someone's ego down to nothing before they will start looking to you for salvation. Then you have a chance to build them back up, showing them that it's your program that takes them from darkness to hope. While you want them to feel good about themselves eventually, you want them to feel that it's because of *you*. They begin to see you as their champion, their hero—even if the weakness you rescue them from is one you created.

LAW 6

When Pimpin' Begins, Friendship Ends

There is little friendship in the world,
and least of all between equals. —Sir Francis Bacon

The pimp game is a lonely one. —Gorgeous Dre

THE LIFE

At sixteen I used to roll with this veteran pimp I admired named Aquarius. We were really tight. I even gave him one of my gold chains to wear. We would ride around the track in Milwaukee while he schooled me on the game. I had just one ho, Dirty Red, at the time, and I was looking to get more. Aquarius taught me about knocking a pimp for a ho.

He told me that a ho is not supposed to look at a pimp who is not her own. It's called reckless eyeballin'. If a ho is caught doing so, it means she is ready to choose a new pimp and be knocked. Aquarius taught me how to sweat a ho who was out of pocket, eyeballin' another pimp.

I couldn't wait to test out my new knowledge on the track. I caught this ho, Bridgette, reckless eyeballin' me, and I started sweating her hard. Now, Bridgette was Aquarius's ho, but Aquarius himself taught me that all's fair in the pimpin' game. When we were out together, he even said to me, "If you see one of my bitches out of pocket, knock her!"

I took him up on it. "Say, bitch," I said to Bridgette. "That nigga you're with will probably need a walker and some bifocals in two years. He's a senior citizen. You need to get with this young pimpin' over here." Bridgette was eighteen. I was sixteen and Aquarius was about twenty-eight, which made him an old man in the game. She liked that I was young and bold.

"Me and you are both young," I told her. "We can get this money. In ten years we can be riding in Benzes and living in mansions."

She said, "I want to fuck with you. You're cute, and you're my age."

I told her to get in my car. At this point, I was driving a Cadillac. I didn't have a legal license, but I had been driving since I was twelve, and I had enough money to buy my own car. I told Bridgette to get in the front seat and throw all of her money—which was about four hundred dollars—on the back seat. I went and picked up her shit from where she was staying, and from that moment on she was *my* ho.

I was eager to serve Aquarius. I thought he would be proud of me for using what he taught me. I called him. "Man, I got some news for you, baby, that you're really going to use," I said, very excited. "I got that Bridgette bitch! I told you I was going to be good at this shit!"

There was silence on the other end. "Man, fuck you!" he finally said, and hung up on me. Aquarius was really mad. He wasn't speaking to me, and he started to pour salt on my name, telling the other pimps that I wasn't shit. He started a hate campaign. His reaction was completely un-pimplike. If a pimp gets knocked for his ho, it's because he wasn't paying attention. He's supposed to take it like a man, step up his game, and try to either get his ho back or knock another nigga for his ho. He doesn't get mad, he gets even. Aquarius's attempt to discredit me backfired. I became a legend at the age of sixteen. Getting my first ho, Dirty Red, was beginner's luck (actually, it was a gift). But to knock a veteran pimp was quite an accomplishment. I got so much respect on the street, because I played by the rules. It wasn't personal, it was straight pimpin'.

The Ism

A pimp has allies, mentors, running partners, and agents, but it's impossible for a pimp to have true friends. Friendship requires loyalty, consistency, and love. There is too much treachery in the game for there to be the kind of bond and trust of a friendship.

In business you have to exploit every situation you can—if friendships prevent it, then you are not on even footing with your competition, and you will lose. When people go into business with their friends, they get caught up thinking things should be a certain way because of the friendship. You believe that your friend will have your back and that you will stick together, no matter what happens. But see what happens when that business goes bad. We expect our enemies to attack us, but when a *friend* betrays you, it is twice as devastating—and you are liable to react emotionally instead of intelligently. And when you are so focused on how your so-called friend is treating you, you're ignoring the business at hand. The two don't mix, and they never have.

LAW 7

Pimp the Game

Business? It's quite simple.
It's other people's money. —Alexandre Dumas

It takes real charisma to be able to
start getting millions instead of thousands. —Ice T

THE LIFE

During my years in prison I did a lot of reading, and one of my favorite books was *Only in America: The Life and Crimes of Don King*. I read that Don King used his pimpish ways to become one of the biggest players in the boxing world. Here was a man—a black man, no less—who had been in the joint for killing a man. He was able to come out and not only make a living, but get a whole bunch of people to buy into an image he had created. He made himself into a king not just in name, but all the way to that crazy-ass hair he styled to resemble a crown.

He put together the "Rumble in the Jungle," the legendary fight between Muhammad Ali and George Foreman, which to this day might be in the top five of the greatest heavyweight fights of all time. King went to Muhammad Ali and told him he had millions of dollars for him to fight George Foreman. Ali wanted his title back anyway, so he signed. He went to

Foreman and told him he had millions for him to fight Ali. Foreman believed him, and he signed too. King had shit. Nothing. But he now had a contract with both Foreman and Ali agreeing to fight one another.

He then went to a promoter with the deal and got the backing he said he already had. King then asked, where could he have this fight and get the most attention? He decided on Africa and even got the king of Zaire to give him ten million dollars. King promised to bring in the celebrities, throw parties, and put an international light on the small country. Then King continued to do what he did best—sold the game. He came up with a catchy name: "Rumble in the Jungle." And the rest is history. Don King pimped the game to the fullest and went on to become the greatest promoter in boxing history.

King inspired me to switch my hustle and build my name so I could make money away from the streets. You know a pimp doesn't have a pension, so I had to make my move and utilize all of the tools that I had at my disposal. The year was 1995. I was in Chicago getting my clothes custom-made at Mr. Kay's on Eighty-ninth Street, when a player tried to sell me a VIP ticket to The Players Ball for five hundred dollars.

"Five hundred dollars! Who's going to be at that motherfucker, Michael Jordan?" I asked.

The nigga started rattling off names: "Bishop Don Juan, Rev. Seymour, Ice T, and all of the pimps and hoes."

I told him that I'd be there. I saw an opportunity. I would go there and convince all of those people to come to Milwaukee to *my* Players Ball. Now, I didn't have a Players Ball at this point. It was just an idea, but they didn't know that. I went to the Chicago ball, and like Don King, I convinced all of those pimps and players that they had to come to *my* ball in Milwaukee. After I secured those commitments, I went to my jeweler and played his sucker ass out of some thousands to sponsor my ball. I went to a few more people and got a few thousand more in sponsorship.

Once I got the money, I used it to promote Pimpin' Ken. I bought fifty thousand flyers, ten thousand posters, and got on all of the radio stations in Milwaukee for thirty days straight. Two weeks later the city was hyped, and everyone knew my name. This gave me a lot of power in town, and I didn't have to spend a single dime of my own money.

I had my man in Chicago make a hundred videotapes of the Players Ball in Chi-town, because it showed how clean I was, and it showed me hobnobbing with all of the players, talking a lot of fast money shit, a lot of slick shit. We gave those tapes out to rappers and other high-ranking pimps and players.

My next move after the word got out was to sell my VIP tickets. I had to trump those niggas in Chicago. My VIP tickets sold for $2,500 a pop. The price told everyone that my shit was going to be bigger and better. I used the money from the sale of those tickets to make sure my event *was* bigger and better. I rented out a big ballroom, using top-of-the-line items for everything. I rented limousines, ordered lots of champagne, and had the whole thing catered. I even invited HBO to film the event.

When you watch *Pimps Up, Ho's Down*, you are watching my Players Ball, the one that helped me build the name "Pimpin' Ken." I used HBO's influence to get under Too $hort and Ice T, both of whom I respect. Because of the special, I was able to get them to do my movie, *Pimpology Uncut*. Then other rappers wanted to fuck with me, because they saw their favorite rappers fucking with me. Everybody loves a winner.

At the end of *Pimpology Uncut* I put my number at the bottom of the screen that sent a message out to all rappers: If they needed someone to spit intros and outros, I was their man. The first big-timer to step up was Jermaine Dupri, the multiplatinum producer. This gave me millions of dollars of free publicity. Everybody worked with me after that. They put me on their songs and in their videos, and to the world I became the king of the pimps.

THE ISM

Like Don King, use other people's money, experience, and knowledge to advance your cause. I owe my newfound fame and success to the power of the rap game. You can't turn on the television without seeing how much hip-hop has influenced culture. White, suburban America spends more money on the music and clothes than black kids do, and many people in Germany and Japan know the lyrics of just about every rap song. Even TV commercials are hip-hop—from the fashion industry to technology. I flipped from pimpin' on hoes to pimpin' on hip-hop, which in turn has pimped on America and the entire world.

LAW 8

Don't Let Your History Be a Mystery

It was my destiny to live a pimp legacy.
—Too $hort, "Where They At?"

THE LIFE

Just like any other field, pimpin' has a history. When I was young, this OG, Jim Dandy, used to tell me about all of the older pimps from back in the day. He talked about pimps that were twenty-five hoes deep with three and four Cadillacs. He would go on and on about them. I let him reminisce and finally asked, "So, where are they now?"

"It's a mystery to me," he said. The only one who remembered anything about these so-called great pimps was Jim Dandy. They hadn't left behind a legacy. They hadn't done anything to keep their names alive.

From that point on I made sure that everything I did would be a history-making event. Once I got my pimpin' right, I threw an annual birthday party. I went out and got the biggest names in the game to celebrate with me. All of the top-flight players—even the ones who really didn't know me—showed up because word got around that my party was *the* party of the year. If you were somebody, you had to be there. Soon niggas were telling people, "I'm kicking it with my boy, Pimpin' Ken." They didn't even know me. Everybody was talking about my party. I threw this party twelve years straight—each year it was bigger and better than the year prior. There are people who were at that first party twelve years ago who are *still* talking about it.

When I did *Pimps Up, Ho's Down*, I made sure I stood out and my shine was on. I gave a performance for the ages. I remember talking to my father afterward and he said, "Man, what the fuck are you doing?" He told me people would now be watching my every move. Why did I want to make myself a target?

"Unless you've been living under a rock, you can see my every move has been to keep my name out there," I explained to him. "And because of that, I will go down in history as the greatest pimp to ever live."

THE ISM

Of all of the things in the world, history is the only one that can record a man's life. What is the point of living if no one remembers that you were ever here? When you do something, *do* the damn thing—do it big or don't do it at all. When you check out, make sure they remember your name. Make sure you have done enough—good or bad— to keep them talking.

LAW 9

Learn the Rules

Business is the art of extracting money from another man's pocket without resorting to violence. —Max Amsterdam

Now, Mr. Pretty Tony, you know the rules of the game. Your bitch just chose me! —Goldie, *The Mack*

THE LIFE

When I was a kid, the movie *The Mack* hit theaters. It was so big that everyone was skipping school just to check out this fly shit—not that I needed an excuse to skip school back then. It starred my man, Max Julien, who was my idol. *The Mack* was shot in Oakland, California, and it represented real pimpin'. It changed the whole game. This was the first time the words "rules" and "pimpin'" were mentioned together on a national level. After that pimps started talking about the rules all the time.

The funny thing about this game, though—no one wants to teach you shit. Veteran pimps don't want the young pimps to know anything, because that will threaten their pimpin'. So you have to find out the rules by hook or by crook. I would try to siphon some rules off of the OGs. I hooked up with this one pimp who was a junkie, but he had plenty of respect and game. His name was Ray, and I would catch him when he was high and not really paying attention to what I was up to. I used to catch him off-guard a lot and got some real pimpin' from the dude.

"Say, Ray, I know how to send the bitch to work, but I know there are some unwritten rules. What are they?" I asked him. "Why don't you hip me to what's happening?"

"Man, you can't take another man's bitch without calling him first," he told me in that raspy dope voice. "That's called serving him. You can't fight over a ho. Don't hang out with busters. That's mis-pimpin'." He was just rattling off the rules like he had memorized them for a test, and I was taking mental notes.

"If a pimp is ho-less and he's a good pimp, give him a jug," he said. "Hook him up. Don't let your bitch hang out with another pimp's ho unless you're putting your ho on that bitch to take her from that pimp. When you're in the presence of other pimps and hoes, make your hoes hold their heads down so they won't be out of pocket." I stopped him.

"Ray, man, write that shit down for me," I said. "I love that shit!"

He said, "Man, you can't write this shit down! Suppose you lose it and one of these squares finds it?"

"You're right, you're right," I said. "Please continue."

But it was too late. I had sobered his ass up with my dumbness. "The game is to be sold, not told," he said. "Stay in it long enough, and you will get from *A* to *Z*. Right now, you just got the *ABC*."

When I started in the game, I was fortunate to have a few mentors—like my man, JD, who gave Dirty Red to me—take me under their wings and teach me the rules of engagement: how to knock a ho, how to instruct a ho, how to build a stable, and so on. But Dirty Red let me in on some trade secrets that I took and ran with. Who better to teach how to pimp a ho than a veteran ho herself? She really taught me that this game is won between the ears, not between the legs. It's not about fucking, it's about fucking with the mind. She taught me more than any pimp would. Dirty Red didn't really think about what she was doing when she schooled me in this game. I was only sixteen and didn't look like any serious threat. She felt a certain amount of power, me being green and all, and took pleasure and pride in seeing me come up. It reflected well on her, but she created a monster.

THE ISM

You'll hear me say that this is the NPA, not the NBA. This is the National Pimpin' Association, a noncontact sport. The NBA bills itself as noncontact, but there is more pushing and shoving, fighting and carrying on, than a little bit. In the NPA, if you come with all of that shit, you're out. The worst pimp is a pimp who doesn't know pimpin'—pimpin' is psychological warfare, it's not physical combat. Pimpin' is a straight mind game.

Every game has rules, and you'd be crazy to think you

can come into it without knowing them. The best players are the ones who not only learn the rules, but master and manipulate them, and then come up with a few rules of their own. You have to have the ability to move and shake like a chess player. You might make a move today, but what you're really doing is setting yourself up ten moves ahead.

LAW 10

Plan Your Work and Work Your Plan

Most of the important things in the world have been accomplished by people who have kept on trying when there seemed to be no hope at all. —Dale Carnegie

THE LIFE

There was this guy named James, a petty hustler. He told me that an Arab grocery store had fifty thousand dollars stashed in the back of the store. All we had to do, he said, was sneak in and snatch the money. When we got inside, there was only three hundred dollars. I was so mad that I punched James in his face, and I didn't give him his share of the loot.

I later realized the situation was actually my fault, and I learned two valuable lessons: one, make sure that you have a real plan that is well thought-out; two, never follow someone else's plan unless you have checked it out for yourself. From that point on, I decided that whatever I did, *I* would investigate it thoroughly. I would weigh all of the consequences and all of the options before I moved on a situation. Some would say I took this planning thing to the extreme, like when I used to make the hoes in my stable write down shit like this:

1. I WILL BE THE BEST HO I CAN BE.
2. I WILL BELIEVE IN MYSELF AND REMAIN
   CONFIDENT IN MY HO'ING.
3. I WILL MAKE AS MUCH MONEY AS I CAN FOR
   KEN TO INVEST IN OUR FAMILY.
4. I WILL NOT FIGHT, CROSS, OR STEAL FROM
   MY WIFE-IN-LAWS.

One day, one of the hoes asked me, "Daddy, why do you make us write down all this shit?"

"Because my plan is to make sure all you bitches act in accord," I told her. "If it's on paper and you read it twice a day, there won't be no excuses."

When I got into the entertainment business, I had to rewrite all of my plans and set a course to take over *that* game. It took me ten years for my plan to come together, but I never thought about quitting. I started off wanting to be respected like my daddy, and I hung around the players until I got that respect. Then I wanted the clothes, jewelry, and cars, and I got all of that shit. Last, I wanted to be in entertainment, but I thought, *What got me here won't get me there.* So I made a new plan and worked it, and here I am today.

THE ISM

They say if you fail to plan, you plan to fail. Without a road map or navigation system, you will get lost. Every plan starts with a vision, then a blueprint, then execution.

It's not enough to have a plan, though; you have to work that plan until you succeed.

Most people don't see their plan out to the end. If something's not working or if it's not happening fast enough, they abandon everything. Instead, be persistent and come up with a new plan. If that plan fails, come up with another one, until you do succeed. You will learn from the mistakes and the things that didn't go right, and that puts you much farther along than if you had no plan in the first place. The only way you lose is if you quit. If you know what you want and you don't give up, you will *always* get it.

LAW 11

Avoid Gorillas and Godzillas

Back up from them like the O'Jays and spin away
like the Bar-Kays. —Pimpin' Ken

THE LIFE

There was this one guy, G-Money. I knocked his ho and called him to serve him the news that would give him the blues.

"Yeah. Yeah. Whatever, man. Fuck that!" he said, sounding very angry.

"Man, these are the rules," I said to him, expecting he would honor the game.

"Nigga, I don't follow no rules," he said. "I'm my own man!"

In pimpin' this is what we call Magilla Gorillas and Godzillas. A real pimp is a gentleman, but these are pimps in gorilla suits. They hang around pimps, they have hoes on the track working for them, they may even *look* like pimps, but they are straight simps. The Magilla Gorilla wants to fight you or kill you if you knock him for his ho. If a ho doesn't bring him his dough, he will beat her without mercy. When he knocks you for your ho, he doesn't serve you, and he will knock a ho who isn't even trying to choose him. He may just snatch that ho up off the track and kidnap her because he wants her. A Magilla Gorilla brings the police to the track with his sucker-ass behavior. In the pimp game this motherfucker has no place, and he's got to go. The Magilla Gorilla plays checkers, but a real pimp plays chess—he uses patience and intelligence to set up the gorilla to take a fall.

I couldn't force G-Money to follow the rules, but I sure as hell wasn't going let him gorilla me either. After you knock a nigga's ho, you're supposed to give a pimp action at a ho, to give him a chance to win her back. This is to ensure that she's not making a "mad move" and choosing you just to get back at her pimp for some grudge. But I decided *not* to give action to a gorilla. Because he wouldn't let it go, it was best to just move that ho to another city. He might grab her off the street and beat her to death. One by one, me and my fellow pimps took away all of G-Money's hoes and put him out of business.

The Ism

Gorillas and Godzillas are bad for the game. They are bad business, and as such, they *have* to go. This is one instance where the real pimps may work together to take care of the situation. In pimpin', to get rid of a gorilla, you have to take away his hoes and move them around, so he doesn't have access to them. Without a ho, a pimp ain't really pimping. And without a ho, a gorilla is just a mean, ugly motherfucker.

In life there are always people who can't help but mess things up for everybody. They are bullies with no finesse, who don't follow any rules. They have no respect for authority or anyone else. They have no principles outside of doing what they feel like at all times. When you see these people coming, you either have to do like E 40 says and "be a professional sucker ducker," or you have to get rid of them. A big enough gorilla may think that nobody can take him out—that he can get away with anything. But even the biggest gorillas can be taken down. Look what they did to motherfucking King Kong!

LAW 12

Ain't No Love in This Shit

*The biggest mistake a bitch can make is to think
that a pimp really loves her.* —Ice T

THE LIFE

A pimp friend of mine, Sly, told all of his hoes that it's
straight pimpin' with him, and the only thing he loves is
cash and more of it. One by one his hoes came and went,
until he was left with just one ho. He sat down this one ho
and said, "It's just you and me now. I want to tell you
something that's been on my mind for a long time. Baby, I
love you."

"What?" the ho said.

"Baby, I love you."

"Daddy, snap out of it!" she said. "Ain't no love in this
game! You're a pimp, and I'm a ho. When I'm through with
you, I will either get a new pimp or get me a square who
knows nothing about my past." Sly looked at this ho and
realized that pimpin' is a lonely game, with no emotions, no
commitments, and no love.

When Sly told me about his dilemma, I had to refresh

his memory about the game. "Pimp, you sell real estate—*ho*-tels," I told him. "If you put feelings over money, you're in the wrong game."

"You're right," Sly said. "Ken, have you ever loved a ho?"

"I love all hoes as long as they give me fresh money," I told him. "But this is love for the game, not some square shit."

He didn't believe me. "Man, come on! You've had some fine-ass hoes, and I know you had to love a few of them."

"Man, I only like a bitch's looks when they keep the tricks hooked. I like the way the pussy feels, but I like it better when it pays Ken's bills!"

THE ISM

It ain't often that I speak of love, but when I do, it's pimpin' I'm speaking of. Ain't no love in this shit. A real pimp only wants a woman to "work, work, work till that pussy hole squirt." He doesn't give a fuck about nothing but the money. As soon as a ho stops paying, a pimp will stop playing. People in certain jobs get training to allow them to do things without thinking about how it affects people, and a pimp has special training too. When I was very young, I trained my mind never to fall in love. In this game you learn to deal with the shit without putting your feelings in it. If you catch feelings, your pimp game is done!

If any business is going to be successful, the bottom line must be the only thing you commit to. Love, feelings, emotions, and happiness are irrelevant when it comes to making money. Money is all that matters—when a stock drops, you drop the stock.

LAW 13

Pimp Like You're Ho-less

One ho is too close to no ho, and broke is
a motherfucking no-no. —Rob Roberson

THE LIFE

A true Milwaukee pimpin' legend, Rob Roberson, once
gave me some very valuable advice: "Pimpin' got you here,
and pimpin' will keep you here," he told me. "No matter
what you do, stay down, and keep working at these hoes.
Get deep, but in order to stay deep, you got to work at a
bitch 24/7. You got to have bitches that you're going to
fuck with later lined up and ready to go. You got to work
the square clubs, the strip clubs, anywhere the hoes party.
Even if you got fifty hoes, it's never enough. Because hoes
come and hoes go." He told me about this one ho he had, a
red-haired white ho who was checking money like the
house was on fire. She was dropping it like it was hot, and
Rob was picking it up like it was not. This red-haired ho
was making so much money that Rob was living large.

He became content and complacent. One day the ho
just up and left. He said he was so lost in the ho money that

he couldn't understand it. He was confused and completely taken by surprise. He did not see that coming. She was his only ho, and he was left ho-less and doughless. Rob is now in his fifties, and he will still tell a young pimp, "Don't get content with one ho. If you're going to pimp, work until your career is over."

THE ISM

I always expected a ho to leave. I pimped like I was ho-less, always in hot pursuit of a new prostitute, and fuck what my other hoes think. It's pimp say, not ho say. I was pimpin' for bread and meat, and if I didn't pimp, I didn't eat.

In the same way, you have to work each day like you're never going to make another dollar. Don't just rely on one stream of income, never put all of your eggs in one basket, and always have backup plans for your backup plans. No matter what your situation, work as if you were working for yourself—because, at the end of the day, you are. Constantly look for other options and opportunities outside your main income, because if you have other options, then you never have to worry about any one thing. When people sense that you're not worried, it makes them respect you more. Whenever you are desperate—and this goes for everything—people will take advantage of you, every time. Make sure you're not dependent on one particular job, person, or income for your security.

LAW 14

Better a Turnout Than a Burnout

*Put some wheels on your heels and rollerskate
the fuck on out of here.* —Pimpin' Ken

THE LIFE

My first ho, Dirty Red, was not just a veteran, she was on
the brink of burning out. Being young in the game, I didn't
know this. I just thought that bullshit automatically came
with a ho and all hoes were trying to run game. She would
say shit like, "Daddy, I don't feel well." Being green, I
asked her if I could get her some soup or take her to the
doctor. "No, I just want to lay with you," she would say.
Feeling sorry for the ho, I would lay with her. It took me
five hoes to understand what was going on. I was pimpin'
on leftover ho'ing. I was really trying to pimp behind
someone else's mess.

I had this one burnout who was only making four hundred dollars a night for her last pimp. I knew she was too
fine to make that little, so I pulled her aside and said,
"Baby, if you can make four hundred dollars in four hours,
I will spend the rest of the night with you." That ho went

to the track and worked really hard, and she came back in four hours with the four hundred dollars. That told me she had been lazy-ass ho'ing—she could have been making that money all along. "Bitch, you been cheating yourself instead of treating yourself," I said. "Now get your ass back out there, and get me eight hundred dollars more!" I had no intention of spending the evening with her—I just needed to confirm that she was indeed trying to play me.

When I first started out in the game, I would have put a wig on a pig to get it a gig. As long as the ho was ho'ing, I would have taken her blind, crippled, or crazy—just as long as she wasn't lazy. She could be black, white, spotted, or dotted—as long as she got it. I didn't realize then how important it would be to my pimpin' to get rid of the burnouts and replace them with some turnouts. When I finally did turn out a ho myself, I realized how much better it was. I was on my block when this girl named Kim, who I went to school with, came up to me and asked me about my work.

"What do you do?" she asked.

"I sell salmon and peel bananas," I told her.

She grabbed her face and said, "Oh my God! You're a pimp, ain't you?"

I grabbed my dick and said, "You're a ho, ain't you?"

"Damn, Ken, what's your problem?" Kim said.

"I only have one problem. I'm tired of all of these tired bitches that I have. I need someone new to be down with me," I said, not really expecting her to take the bait.

She paused for a moment and then said, "What do I need to do to join?"

"Bitch, this is not an army!" I told her. "You can't *join*. You got to sell some pussy, get me some money, and make it official like a referee's whistle!" This was the first time that I had ever seen stars in a woman's eyes. The burnouts I had weren't impressed by nothing, but Kim hung on every word I said. Not only did Kim eventually come to make me a lot of money, but she helped me hone my pimpin' skills. I was able to mold and shape her the way I needed. She ho'd the way I taught her to ho. She did things exactly the way I wanted them done.

The Ism

They say that pimps perspire and hoes expire. A burnout is a ho that has expired—her time is up, like a cigarette with no butt. She's been with every pimp on the track, she's cynical, conniving, and mad, and she will try to ruin everything around her. If she's in a stable, she will try to fuck it up and run the other hoes off. She's on her last leg, and she always wants to start some shit. When this happens, a pimp must find a turnout—something fresh off the press. Ain't no nigga mis-pimped on her, ain't no nigga poisoned her. The only pimpin' she'll know is *his* pimpin', and he can groom her from *A* to *Z*.

It's a lot easier to teach someone the way you want things done than it is to unteach someone else's bad habits. No one wants to hear, "Well, at my other company, we did things this way . . ." or "My old boyfriend used to do this for me . . ." They want someone eager to learn and eager to please. Most people come into a situation with baggage and bad habits, but if they aren't willing to leave the bags at the door, then you can't let them in. When people get fed up with their jobs, their lives, or their love lives, they can become bitter. Because misery loves company, these people will try to make everyone around them miserable. A few feet is the only difference between a rut and a grave, and they will try to drag you into the grave with them. Get rid of the burnouts in your life— you can't help them, they have to help themselves.

LAW 15

Say What You Mean and Mean What You Say

*They're going to test you, man. Whatever you say
out your mouth, they're going to make sure you stand by that.*
—Bishop Don Magic Juan

THE LIFE

When I was about ten years old, I took a hundred dollar
bill from my daddy's dresser. My friends and I spent it all
on candy. My daddy came to me a few days later and asked
me if I took the money. Knowing my daddy was crazy and
was going to whip my ass, I quickly said, "No sir!"

He got down to my level and looked me in the eye.

"Boy, I want you to tell me the truth," he said. "Say
what you mean and mean what you say, because if you lie, I
will tear your little ass up!"

I took a gamble. "Yes, I took it," I said.

My pops smiled at me. "All a man's got is his word and
his honor," he said.

I thought about that years later, when my bottom bitch
reminded me of some shit I had totally forgotten. I had told
her that she could be with her mother on Christmas. How-
ever, at the time, I was on a mission for a new Benz. If I let

her go home, the rest of the stable would have wanted to go home also. This was one of those times when your honor is put to the test. I had to play this just right. "Bitch, go home and have fun," I told her. "I said you could go, and I meant it, so good-bye. But me and these other bitches are going to stay on the road and get this Benz."

The ho thought about it for a minute. "Okay, Daddy," she said. "Since you kept your word, I'll stay and help you get that Benz."

The Ism

No matter how much of a hustler my father was, there were still certain rules that applied, even on the street. Saying what I meant, and meaning what I said, was one of them. It didn't prevent me from getting what I wanted, and it actually came in handy. I knew that ho had a competitive spirit, so I used it to my advantage. She wasn't going to let those other hoes buy the Benz without her contributing. I found a way to get what I wanted without going back on my word, which probably would have backfired. I would have lost the trust of this one ho, and I would have looked untrustworthy to the whole stable. Hoes will test you to the end, so if I said I was going to do something, I made sure it got done. When I said we were going to The Players Ball, we went. If I said I was going to buy a new car, it got bought. Saying what I meant, and meaning what I said, got me out of an ass-whipping *and* it got me a new Benz.

Whatever you tell a person, you better think about it before it comes out of your mouth. Because if you say it, you have to deliver. They say honesty is the best policy. That doesn't mean you have to tell the whole truth, but you must always keep it real—with yourself, if no one else. Lying shows a lack of character and an inability to face reality. There are better ways to manipulate someone than to lie.

LAW 16

Give Motivation and Inspiration

*Let me take you to the pot of gold
at the end of the rainbow.* —Pimpin' Ken

THE LIFE

For about one thousand dollars, I could get beautiful fur coats off the street that would retail for ten thousand dollars. I also had a deal with a local furrier, where I would bring in my coat and for a G, he would take my coat, put a ten-thousand-dollar price tag on it, and hang it up with his coats. I would tell a ho that I was going to buy her a fur. I may have been teasing her with this for a few weeks. Finally, I would take her to the furrier to pick one out. I would steer her in the direction of *my* coat. I would tell her that it was the perfect coat for her, that it made her look really nice. The furrier would join in, telling her how fly she looked in it. I said she could have any coat in the store, but she naturally gravitated to the coat I had selected for her. When she looked at the price tag, she really flipped for it. I would give the furrier a thousand in front of my ho. I would tell her, "I just put a G down on *your* coat. Every week, I will put another G on the coat, until it's paid for. At the end of ten weeks, you will be wearing your coat. You'll be the baddest bitch at The Players Ball!"

That ho would be on the track ho'ing like crazy to bring me that money to buy that coat. After two weeks, I broke even, and the other eight weeks just lined my pockets. But even more valuable to me was that my ho was a happy fucking camper. Thinking about that coat made her job easier, and it made my household more peaceful. Having the coat as motivation also helped me keep the ho in line. If she started getting out of pocket, I would hold that coat over her head and threaten her with not getting it.

If it wasn't a fur, it was jewels. Pimps always have access to expensive shit that "falls off trucks." On the street I could get diamonds and platinum jewels for a tenth of the price. I had a deal with a local jeweler as well, who would "sell" my jewels to my hoes and mark up the price. We had our own special ho layaway plan.

The Ism

It's important that a ho doesn't feel like she's ho'ing for nothing. She has to constantly have an incentive, a carrot dangled in front of her face. A pimp has to keep her distracted with the things she thinks she wants, and he has to constantly fill her head with more and more things for her to want.

People work to survive, but they only work hard when they want something really bad—a new car, a new house, a college fund for their children—and they are shown a means to get it. In corporate America they dangle raises, bonuses, and commissions over a worker's head, even though it's just money they should have been paying him all along. Without these games, he might have the motivation to get up every day, go to that job, and do the minimum not to get fired, but the incentives inspire him to really hustle.

LAW 17

Get You a Bottom Bitch

One bad bitch beats five funky hoes.
—King James

THE LIFE

I had one ho who took my pimpin' for eight years. She would get up every day and go to work, sometimes for ten to twelve straight hours. She would go to sleep just to wake up to get a pimp some more money. This ho was in it to win it. Not only did she motivate the next worthy ho who wanted to rise in the game, but she set the standard for my pimpin'. I called her Ivy, because she made me a much better pimp. She helped me elevate my pimpin'. I would talk to her about my plans for myself and for her. I would write down my plan on paper, and I would make her read my plan every day. I talked to her until I was blue in the face. It was my duty to instill in her the drive to get money and let her know that once she commits to this game, it's a part of her. She had to eat, sleep, and shit my pimpin', until she believed in everything I was telling her. If I told her something was going to happen, in her mind it was already done.

The Ism

A bottom bitch is important to a pimp's success. She has a purpose—to see her pimp rich and on top. A pimp may have only one good ho in his career. He may have five hoes, and four of them will be his motherfucking cheerleaders, but one—that bottom bitch—is the one he will win with. She's the one who will school all of the other hoes to a pimp's ways. She'll let the other hoes know that if they're not down with the pimp and his ways, they have to leave. Because a bottom bitch is so important to a pimp's game, he has to watch her carefully. As soon as he sees a glimpse of her being disgruntled, he has to hand over her walking papers. So that he can replace her when the time comes, it's also important to keep a bottom bitch-in-waiting.

To win in life, you need to have a solid team of people around you, and the people closest to you have to be really down for you. As the leader of the team, you need to focus ten moves ahead, and you can't do that if you're dealing with every little thing. A team captain handles things for you, leads the other players, and gives them an example to look up to. A strong captain communicates your vision, enforces it, and inspires your team to really want to win.

LAW 18

Cop and Blow

Man, bitches come and go, every nigga pimpin' know.
—50 Cent, "P.I.M.P."

THE LIFE

Back in the late 1970s and early 1980s, you could see one ho go through ten pimps. And all the pimps would say, "The name of the game is cop and blow, and the loser has to watch the ho go."

There was this one pimp, who didn't quite go with this flow. His name was Fly from D.C. Every pimp knew that his ho was fair game to any other pimp, but Fly wasn't having it. I was out there doing my thing, and I saw this fine white ho working the blade. I got down at the ho, and I sweated her all night. Finally, a real dark brother pulled up to me.

"My man, can you pull over?" he said. "I need to talk to you."

We met at the gas station on M Street. When we got there, he got out of the car and came over to me. "Man, you been sweating that ho all night and didn't get any action," he said. "Can you let her get my money?"

"Nigga, you don't know? The name of the game is cop and blow," I reminded him.

"I see you've been reading them Iceberg Slim books," he said. "But the book I read says, it's 'cop, lock and *block*.' I don't mean no disrespect, but this is how I eat on these streets. So if you can, let that ho make my money." I kind of liked the guy, so I stopped sweating that ho.

Two weeks later he blew the ho. We talked again, and he said, "I should have kept it in the family and let you get that ho. The bitch got out on me."

"Man, what you talking about?" I said. "I thought she was solid."

"The ho blew up," he said. I laughed, and that's when I came up with the term "ho up or blow up."

"I've been in this shit for a long time, and I done seen a lot of hoes come and go," I said. "This game is funny. A ho may pay you for two days or a ho may pay you for twenty years, but these hoes stay the same. You can cop one, and you can blow one."

THE ISM

A pimp learns that he can't get too caught up in a ho, and he certainly can't feel bad when he loses one. Cop and blow is gaining and losing hoes with grace. If a pimp knows the game, he knows he will lose a ho, maybe his best ho. But he has to keep it moving, like it's nothing. He has to let it roll off his back, because there will always be another ho to take that ho's place. If he can't handle losing hoes, he might as well just get out of the game.

In life you will have gains and losses, successes and failures. What determines your fate is how you handle them. Those who know that life comes with ebbs and flows, and that you have to ride those waves, will be successful. You have to be able to roll with the punches, take what comes at you, and have enough inside to brush the dirt off your shoulder and keep mashin' for your ration.

LAW 19

Turn Ho Ends into Dividends

I'm going from the ghetto streets to the executive suites, from the ghetto blocks to Wall Street stocks, from the sewer to an entrepreneur, from ho tracks to the office fax. —Pimpin' Ken

THE LIFE

When I was a youngster, my daddy always told me, "Son, don't go broke!" It seemed like real simple advice, like common fucking sense. Like most knuckleheads on the streets, I didn't listen. I thought, *I got this!* I would go on the streets, put down a hustle or two, and spend my money as soon as I got it. Because I didn't save my money, I found myself deeper and deeper in the game, which led to stealing and eventually landed me in the joint.

I met some of the smartest men while I was in jail, but there was one thing these motherfuckers had in common. As intelligent as they were, they—like me—didn't have a game plan, and that's what landed them there. One of the OGs in the joint was trying to get his shit together. He would always have a book in his hand. One day I walked up to him and said, "Nigga, you think you're so smart, don't you?" He looked at me like he wanted to do something, but he recognized that he had been in the joint long enough. He knew nothing good could come of talking slick to a young hothead like me.

He smiled and said, "Young man, I heard about you. I know you tried your hand at pimpin'. For that reason, I will tell you a little story about my life before I came to jail. About fifteen years ago I was ten deep. Ten hoes—a hundred toes, in case you didn't know. I had a brand-new Cadillac and was getting forty Gs a week. I owned three mansions and went shopping like a Muslim prays: five times a day. I had ten sets of jewelry—I changed jewelry ten days a week. I had my own mink farm, because they couldn't kill the little sonafabitches fast enough to supply me and all my hoes for winter. My pimp friends used to *beg* me not to compete for Pimp of the Year at The Players Ball, so that they'd have a chance to win. My cash stash was in the millions. Then it all changed. One day, one of my hoes got out of pocket. I hit the bitch in the head, and the ho fell dead. I had the other hoes hide the body while I got out of town. I tried to pimp long distance, but every one of those hoes left me. I used every dime trying to hide from the law. For five years I ran without a plan, spending them ho ends. Not once had I ever thought about investing that ho money. If I had done that, maybe I wouldn't be in the joint today."

He then handed me a book. It was *Think and Grow Rich* by Napoleon Hill. "Take this book," he said. "This book will change your life and uplift your pimpin' to a level these suckers will never understand. Pimp on a ho until the wheels fall off the Benz, but at the same time, take your money and invest it in a business, in real estate, or open up some type of store."

After I got released from jail, I took that OG's advice and got my money right. I opened up a grocery store and a clothing store, and I invested in real estate. I started a film company and a management company. Now I'm an OG, but I don't have to go through the shit that OG went through.

THE ISM

Most players in the hustle live for the right now, instead of letting their next move be their best move. All of my brothers on the block, with rocks in their socks, get caught—they sell that dope for three years and then do thirty in the joint. The smart move would be to make that money, take that money, and then flip that shit. Pimps don't have pensions or social security. There's no pimp retirement fund. A pimp must turn ho ends into dividends. You can either "pimp or die," or invest and multiply.

You need to have an endgame. Turn your dollars into hoes, so that your money will be working for you, instead of you working for it. Have that money out on the track, breaking itself every single day. The wealth you have today can be gone tomorrow, if you don't invest and prepare for the future. Even the Bible tells a story that concludes, "I tell you that to everyone who has, more will be given, but as for the one who has nothing, even what he has will be taken away." You not only have to avoid spending all your money, but even just saving it is not enough—you have to *grow* your wealth.

LAW 20

Get In a Ho's Head

Control is the soul. —Pimpin' Snooky

THE LIFE

My first ho, Dirty Red, had ten pimps before me. That *did*
make her a pro, and she had this game down pat. "Ken, if
you ask a bitch to do something, and she acts like she
doesn't hear you, or she snaps, 'What?' that's a good indi-
cation that she's ready to leave," Dirty Red told me.

"Smart-ass bitch, how you know that?" I asked. "You
ain't never pimped on a ho." There I was, sixteen years old,
never pimped on a ho, and I was questioning this veteran.
She thought for a minute, and I assumed she was thinking,
*I'm only trying to lace this young-ass pimp, and he is getting
offended?* I was so insecure about what I didn't know that I
was getting mad at her for trying to school me. But I
calmed down quick, because if I was going to be a king in
pimpin', I needed that game.

Finally, she put her hands on her hips and said, "Daddy,
I'm a ho, and that's what we do when we get tired of a

nigga pimp." I realized that no one knows what a ho is thinking better than a ho.

So I said, "Okay, bitch, what else?" I became her willing student, but I still had to be in control. Dirty Red told me that a woman will almost always lie about an orgasm. I didn't really care whether a ho had an orgasm or not, but you never know when knowledge will come in handy later.

"If you lay some good dick, you will know if it's the real thing," she said. "A bitch will pant your name, roll over like a puppy, and go to sleep in broad daylight, shaking all the while. Most simps go for the fake and think they can control a bitch with the dick, but if you allow yourself to be faked out like that, then you are the one who is being controlled by the pussy. In the game a pimp who can be faked out is tender in the zipper, and a bitch will have no respect for him."

Another ho of mine, Ivy, showed me that women have a hunger to shop, and if I fed it, I would eat forever. She loved to shop so much that I could manipulate her with shopping. If she thought about being out of pocket, she knew that her shopping days would be cut short. It actually kept her in line. All I would have to say was, "Do you want to go shopping?" and she'd smile when she felt like frowning. That lesson came in handy when I knocked this other ho from an old-school pimp named Nate. She was a hardworking ho. One day she caught a trick for some big money, and I gave her a G to go shopping. As I handed her the ten crisp hundred-dollar bills, she started to cry. "What's the matter with you, bitch?" I said, really puzzled. "I just gave you a G!"

"I love shopping," she said. "But the guy I used to be with never let me shop on my own." That pimp would buy his hoes everything—from clothes to tampons. He wouldn't let them have a dime to shop on their own. These women informed me that it's the small things in life that count when it comes to a woman. The kind words, or bringing her a gift for no reason, or remembering her birthday or something special to her, and listening when she talks—those things really matter to them.

Most pimps would think, "You must be out of your mind!" Pimps just don't do that square shit. Pimps never treat a ho with much kindness, but I took this lesson and made it work for me. It took my pimpin' to a whole other level. Unless she feels love for you, a ho's not going to give you her money for eight- and ten-year stretches. Some hoes want you to be hard on them, but with others it's like Pimp C says, "You serve vinegar, you gonna get pickles"—the trick is to figure out each ho's mind.

I knew one ho named Jazzy Dezi, a twenty-three-year-old all-American snow bunny. She told me, "Most hoes are lost little girls who have been neglected growing up, now living in a woman's body. Hoes don't do this because they enjoy turning tricks, most hoes don't even like sex. They believe a pimp will give them the love and care they didn't have growing up. A ho does not want to be told the same thing a pimp tells all his other hoes, especially a bottom bitch. This is why bottom bitches run off the other hoes. In her mind a pimp is a ho's man, and yet she has to work with other girls that think the same thing. You have to remember, us hoes are women before we are hoes."

THE ISM

As I have always said, the book on what a ho will do has yet to be written. You can never really know everything that goes on inside a ho's head, but one of things that made me such a good pimp was that on some level, I understood a lot about what made a ho tick. My best teachers? Hoes! Over the years I learned some valuable lessons and gained a lot of insight from the hoes I had around me.

Knowledge is power, and it's available to anyone willing to really pay attention. When people tell you what they think and what makes them tick, it's to your advantage to learn as much as you possibly can. Ask them what their dreams are, and really listen to their answers. Then you can use that information to make *your* dreams come true.

LAW 21

A Ho Without Instruction
Is Headed for Self-Destruction

If you knew better, you'd do better. —Jim Jones, "Credibility"

You bought a one-way ticket to something bigger than you.
—Bun B, "Good Stuff"

THE LIFE

One day I was on the track, and this ho who obviously
didn't have any instruction waved me down and told me
I had a nice car. I was pushing a 500 Benz at the time. She
asked me if I wanted to have some fun. This dumb-ass
bitch didn't realize she was fucking with a pimp. I was
in a slick-ass car, wearing blue and white gators, with a
fresh mink and plenty of jewels. How dumb could she be?

"Baby girl, I don't mean no harm, but I'm a pimp," I
told her, feeling a little sympathetic. "If you stand here and
converse with me any longer, I will have to ask you to
break yourself."

"A pimp?" she said, kind of stunned. "I don't fuck with
no pimps!"

"Well, that could be your problem," I said. "You're dis-
obedient with the wrong ingredient. Have you ever seen

Stevie Wonder leading Ray Charles somewhere? You need guidance."

"How are you going to guide me?"

"I'll give you directions to the next intersection," I said. "I can show you brighter days and better ways, with the proper instruction for a bigger production. Before we can do all of this, you got to drop it out of your cock and put it in a pimp's sock. But if you want to be a renegade out here, your ass is out of pocket. A solo ho without a pimp will soon be put under pimp arrest or worse. It's in your best interest to choose a pimp. It's in your best interest to choose Pimpin' Ken."

"I'm confused," she said. "Can I have a little time to think about this?"

Knowing all the other pimps would be up on the green ho, I couldn't give her time to think about shit. "I have seen hoes get killed because they didn't know the best place to turn a date or how to hide a razor blade in her ID or her wig to protect herself against a violent trick. I've seen hoes get beat up by other hoes for playing with some other ho's pimp—talking to him without giving him money, like you're doing right now. I've seen hoes go to jail because a pimp didn't let her know that Tuesdays and Thursdays were vice nights. Do you see these Cadillacs?" I said, pointing to all of the pimp cars lining the track. "They've been sizing you up, talking about how out of pocket you are. As soon as I leave, they will roll up on you and take your money and kick your ass. So now, what do you think I should do with a bitch—should I leave her? Or will she pass that trap like a quarterback to the pimp receiver?" That ho jumped right into my car and broke herself. Not two weeks later, she was laced with so much game that other pimps rode by saying, "Is that the same bitch?"

THE ISM

When you see renegades in any game operating without instruction, you should see an opportunity. It's a good sign when people are in over their heads, because at least they have some hustle. You are in a position to rescue them, because you have the plan and the program they need to avoid self-destruction, but they don't get it for free: The game is sold, not told. You provide the information that gives them the advantage, but in exchange for your knowledge, you are the boss. You don't give them too much knowledge, either—it's a strictly need-to-know basis. That's how you ho them down and keep them around.

LAW 22

Keep Hoes on Their Toes

Habit is either the best of servants or the worst of masters.
—Nathaniel Emmons

THE LIFE

I had a ho named Carmen—a fine, young ho who I didn't want to get out on me. I knew I had to be really tight to keep this ho in check. Every time she got used to a spot, I would tell her to pack up her shit, and I would send her to another city. This cost me a lot of money, but it had a purpose.

Every time she got to a new city, she had to spend the majority of her time learning it. She didn't have time to think about much else. She also depended heavily on me for valuable information. There weren't too many places that I hadn't pimped before, and I knew just about every pitfall and sweet spot. When she wasn't on the track, she spent her time talking to me on the phone. I was her only friend. Once a month I would drop in and check on her. She would look forward to my visits, because she knew that for the day, it would be just me and her. She felt special.

Very few pimps can pimp on this level. You may not see

a ho for weeks at a time, but she still sends you that money. In the game we call this "the automatic." I learned this move from my man, JD. The dude had hoes in many cities. He wouldn't see them but once every three months, and those hoes were breaking themselves automatically. One day before I really got deep in the game, we got into a debate about this. "Man, them hoes are beating the hell out of you!" I said. "They are beating and cheating you. You know damn well they're not sending you the full trap."

"Lil' bro, if a bitch steals a thousand, I still break even," he said. "I would spend more than that on shopping for the bitch, buying food for the bitch, and gas to follow that bitch around, none of which I have to do when she's not here. As long as they think they're beating me by stealing, and they are still sending me something, I'm ahead of the game. They're only really stealing from themselves. The only way I can lose is if the bitch wakes up and says, 'Fuck JD!' and keeps *all* of the money."

Damn, I thought, *he sees this game from a whole other perspective.*

"Pimpin', I play chess with these hoes," he told me. "I move them around like pawns, and I stay checking them."

THE ISM

One of the best ways to keep a ho off balance is to move her around. If a ho is in a location too long, she will get used to the place, and her mind will wander to her own thoughts. She may think she doesn't need a pimp, and why not keep all the money for herself?

Without roots, even the mightiest tree can be easily moved here and there. People are the same way. Without strong ties to a place, family, or loved ones, they can be easily manipulated and controlled. If you can keep a person off-balance, they'll be too busy trying to regain stability to try to unbalance you.

LAW 23

A Ho Joins a Stable to Ruin It

One bad apple can spoil the whole bushel.
—proverb

THE LIFE

Aquarius was one slick pimp with a nice stable of hoes. He told me, "You have to screen a ho to the fullest when she first joins your stable." I was young and had no idea what he was talking about.

I said, "The next ho you knock, why don't you let me sit in on it, so I can see how you put it down, Big Pimpin'?" This nigga was an egomaniac. I knew if I pumped his ego, he'd do anything for me. One day we were riding the track on Martin Luther King Avenue, and he got at one dope-fiend pimp's ho.

"Bitch, your pimp's like Boo-Boo the rabbit—he's got a dope habit!" Aquarius said. "And if you don't make that move, you'll be next. He's going to have you shooting that shit, bitch. Believe that. Come and join my stable, where a ho is always able." She looked at Aquarius, indicating she was down with that move. "That's *my* ho, Young Pimpin'," he said to me.

"Shit if she ain't!" I said. "Man, she was looking at you so hard, I started to wipe her eyeballs off your forehead with this napkin."

He laughed and said, "You are fly as hell for a young pimp." We pulled off. By the time we got to the corner, the ho was waving Aquarius down. He told her to get in the back seat and then he drilled the ho like a drill sergeant:

"Bitch, what's your pimp's number so I can call him and serve him?

"How many kids do you have?

"What's your mama's name?

"Have you ever been with another woman?

"Have you ever stashed money on your pimp?

"What's the most money you ever made at one time?

"Can you get along with other hoes?"

Aquarius asked that ho a hundred and one questions. After he broke her, he served her pimp and put her back down on track. We pulled off and the lesson began.

"Young dog, a ho will wreck a stable in a minute," he said. "I asked her all of those questions to try to get a feel for her. Is she jealous? How does she feel about her mama? If she doesn't love her mama or her kids, a pimp or another ho doesn't stand a chance! When I asked her the most money she made, I asked that so I could see her response. I can look into her eyes and see if her eyes get big, see if she has a love for money. If she likes money, I will put her with my top money-making ho, and they can battle it out to see who can bring in the most. The more questions you ask a ho, the more she talks. The more she talks, the more you find out if she can fit in with your other hoes and if she's fit for your pimpin'."

I had to give it to Aquarius, he knew how to keep his hoes under control. As I got deeper in the game, I was able to execute the valuable game that I got from him. If I screened a ho, and she was a problem ho, I separated her from the good ones. I may not have gotten rid of her, but I definitely did not allow her to mess up my stable.

The Ism

In the pimp game we call a group of hoes a stable, but really there's nothing less stable. It takes a lot of work to keep any household in balance—much less a group of jealous and competitive women sharing one man. The pimp is the boss, and there are two things employees love most: undermining the boss and undermining each other.

It only takes one negative element to ruin all of the hard work of running a smooth operation. You have to prevent negativity from coming in, and if it gets by you, you have to chase it out immediately. You don't play with a bad seed, thinking you can change it. If it sets down roots, it will be that much more difficult for you to pull that sucker up and get rid of it. Is a healthy person going to rub off his good health and make a sick person well? No, it never works that way.

LAW 24

Set the Trend

By the song's end I'll probably start another trend.
—Jay-Z, "30 Something"

THE LIFE

I don't know a cat in the game who set more trends internationally than my man JD. Back in the 1970s, JD and I were the first young dudes in our hood to get our hair pressed. For youngsters who don't know what that business is, we got our hair permed. Just a few weeks later it seemed like the whole hood was on that shit too. He had all of us drinking Moët before a rapper ever rhymed about it. We were wearing designer sunglasses at night before that became popular. JD was always thinking about what he would do next. One time he pulled up with some pictures of us on which he had drawn crowns on our heads. No one in our pimp circle was wearing crowns at that point, but when we started doing it, it took off.

Once I decided that I was truly going to be in the game, the first thing I said was that I was going to set the standards on how niggas put it down. In Milwaukee a lot of the so-called players and pimps were wearing tennis shoes and casual shit. I said, "Fuck that! I'm wearing gators like the vets wear." I had to separate myself from them tennis-shoe–wearing young lames. The next thing I know, everybody switched their style up and started imitating young pimpin'. In *Pimps Up, Ho's Down*, you will see me in a black-and-white mink. After that all of these dudes started rocking the two-tone minks.

In 1993 I was in New York City, and I just bought a Presidential Rolex with the beveled set. I used to frequent the diamond district, and I started buying my jewelry from this dude who had a store right on the corner of Forty-seventh Street. His name was Jakob. Everybody in the rap game was fucking with Tito up the street. I bought my watch and headed up the street to holler at Tito. Standing outside his store was Biggie Smalls and Lil' Cease. They said they were waiting for Puffy to pull up. Biggie saw my watch and was impressed. "Man, that's a cold mother-fucker!" Biggie said. Next thing, he and Lil' Cease went to holler at Jakob. Two years later everybody was fucking with Jakob the Jeweler. When I first started wearing Mauri gators—ten years before I became a spokesman and a model for them—players would come up to me and ask, "What type of gators are you wearing? They are so pimp-ish!" I would tell them they were Mauris. The next thing I knew, everybody was on some Mauri shit. When I first started fucking with these rap cats, there wasn't a single pimp who had appeared on a CD, spitting game or appearing in videos. I didn't do it to start a trend, but that's what happens when you do your best.

THE ISM

A true leader is someone who people want to follow because the person is doing things that no one else is doing. You set the standards and the trends people follow, and it gives you the appearance of being superior to the people who imitate you. Sometimes people will take your style and try to make people think it's really their shit. But you can't get mad, because the people who imitate you, more often than not, want to be you.

Do things in such a way that people want to follow your lead. Don't be a follower. Don't ask, "What happened?" Make shit happen.

LAW 25

Grind for Your Shine

It's lights, camera, and action, you know what I'm sayin'?
—Kenny Red

Pimp so hard, a nigga drag his mink on the floor.
—Puff Daddy, "The World Is Filled ..."

THE LIFE

One of the biggest misconceptions is that a pimp is some-one who wears loud suits and big hats or shoes with glass heels with fish swimming around in them. Those are clowns, not pimps. Everyone loves a clown, but no one wants to take a clown home. When I was pimpin', I looked more like a Wall Street executive than the stereotype of a pimp. When I went casual, I was still classy—Davoucci leather, classic jeans, and Timberlands. A pimp's style is not in the labels, it's just a certain look that stands out. You *can* stand out without looking like a clown, and I always looked for things that were different.

A lot of younger pimps wear things like gator jackets with mink. That's cool, because the probability of a square wearing that are slim to none, and that's what a pimp cares about. He has to distinguish himself from the average Joe on the street. My Davoucci coat costs fifteen hundred dollars, and a ho would know that. I have knocked many a ho in my career simply because of my style. A ho wants to be seen with the flyest nigga on the street, so I made it my business to be that nigga.

THE ISM

It makes a ho feel extra good when her pimp looks extra good. She wants to see something for her investment, and her pimp's shine is how she shows it off. His job is to sell her a dream of glamour, success, and the life she never had. He's got to look the part he's playing.

When you're looking sharp, you'll notice you get more respect than you get otherwise—you gain some luster. This affects how you handle yourself. People tend to act the way they look, so make sure you look like a winner. All successful people understand we are judged by our appearance. The tighter your look, the greater your potential for advancement. If you're trying to reach the top, you'd better pay attention to details—from your haircut down to the heels of your shoes.

LAW 26

The Game Is to Be Sold, Not Told

Those who know, don't tell.
And those who tell, don't know. —Pimp BJ

THE LIFE

The first time I saw somebody get shot, I was a little nigga, about seven years old. It was in front of the Robert Terrell projects in Chicago. Two men were arguing, and one of them pulled out a gun and shot the other in the head, right in front of me. My uncle grabbed me and pulled me into the building.

"Boy, get in the house," he said. "You ain't seen nothing!"

Once I got old enough to really hit the streets, the OGs would always tell me, "Boy, you don't know nothing." The first thing I learned was to keep my mouth shut. If I wanted to know something, I had to watch, listen, and learn.

My boy JD and I would go try to hang around the older players to pick their brains for game. But every time we came around, it seemed like the conversation would switch up. We would hear them talking about shooting dice or the way to break a ho, but as soon as they saw us walk up, all conversation stopped. Even though JD and I were young-sters, these OGs wanted to keep us in the dark.

One day I saw Jim Dandy putting down some game on a lame. He was gambling with this sucker, and for the life of this guy, he couldn't win for shit. Jim Dandy ended up winning all of the sucker's money and sending him home broke. After he left, I went up to Jim Dandy and said, "Put me up on your move, player."

"I know your daddy," he said. "And I like you a lot. But if you ain't up on game, son, I can't wake up the dead."

"Man, I'm up on the game," I said. "I just don't know what *you* did with that sucker."

"You got to pay for what you don't know," he said. "The game is to be sold, not told."

"How much does a young player need?" I asked.

He laughed and said, "Boy, you got to pay with your ass. You got to get played until your ass wakes up and knows for a fact that you've *been* played. This game is full of tricks, and a sucker is born every day. Even a doctor tip-toes past the medicine cabinet, because he doesn't want to wake up the sleeping pills. Until you get your head bumped enough, you will be in the dark."

I spent some years in the dark, bumping my head in the game. But I learned, eventually. Then, when a young pimp came up to *me* for some game, the first thing I'd tell him was, "You got to get this shit like you live, pimp. If the game is for you, homie, you're going to get it anyway."

Really, the less a young pimp knew, the better it was for me—the better chance I had to knock him for his ho. I wanted him to pay in blood, like I had.

The Ism

In the game we're all competing for the same spot—number one. No one wants to share their secrets or their game, because they don't want to give another player an advantage. The less your opponent knows, the better. The only way I'll tell it is if I sell it. If you have ever bought any of my videos or any of the CDs that I've appeared on—better yet, if you bought this book—I have sold you game. The only thing that's free is air. So keep breathing, nigga!

Ignorance is bliss . . . but only for the person with the knowledge. That's why there is so much misinformation and confusion out there. People with the knowledge don't really want those without it to have it. So if you do share it, make sure you get something in return.

LAW 27

Keep Your Game on the Low

An intelligent person can play stupid, but a stupid person can never play intelligent. —Pimpin' Ken

THE LIFE

While I was in the game, I recognized that being on top and staying on top was about control—not just controlling my hoes, but controlling myself and controlling my mouth. For example, I would never let a ho know what I was really thinking, how much money I really had, or how many hoes were really in my stable. I had a trick where I would tell my Milwaukee hoes that I had hoes in New York, Chicago, and Los Angeles. I would even take them with me to Western Union to pick up money from those places—this was money that I had wired myself. But it made my Milwaukee hoes feel special that they got to be with me, while those "other hoes" were breaking themselves from afar.

Good pimps have a gift for gab, but smart pimps talk a lot and at the same time don't say much at all. When I would spin my phrases and twist my words, it was for effect. But I never gave up valuable information. When the HBO producers approached me about doing *Pimps Up, Ho's Down*, I knew how they looked at us. I knew that they looked at all of us pimps as straight fools. But I didn't say anything, I just played along. They came in talking about how they were going to make me a superstar and how the whole world would know my name. I was thinking, *Who the fuck do they think they're talking to? Those are the kinds of lines I use on hoes.* I gave them everything they thought they were looking for. Finally, when they were totally committed to the project and it was time to sign the contracts, I pulled out my list of demands. The producer was looking at me like he had seen King Kong. While they thought they were dealing with a dummy, I was watching their every move and planning mine. I decided if they were going to use me, I was going to use them.

Here were my demands:

1. IF YOU'RE GOING TO DO A MOVIE, I WANT TO SHOOT MY MOVIE AT THE SAME TIME.
2. I WANT MORE MONEY THAN EVERYBODY ELSE.
3. I WANT THE MOVIE TO END WITH ME.
4. I WANT TO BE A CONSULTANT FOR THE MOVIE.

This is how you have to play the game. Keep your shit on the low. When it's time to get the money, show your hand. I received everything I asked for. Check out the credits on *Pimps Up, Ho's Down*. You will see "Pimpin' Ken, consultant." Ha ha!

THE ISM

Everybody hates a know-it-all. Even if you do know it all, it's to your advantage to pretend like you don't. If people think you're stupid, they will underestimate you and relax, which gives you the advantage. The less a motherfucker knows about you, the better. If you talk too much, you will give away information and make yourself vulnerable to attack, so the best approach is to say little and conceal your hustle. If you don't want people to know something, you have to keep your mouth closed. I don't know why, but that seems to be the hardest thing in the world for people to do. There is no such thing as a secret, and if you tell someone anything in confidence, expect for it to get out. On the other hand, if you have some misinformation that you *do* want to get out, go ahead and share it as a secret.

People are more likely to educate and inform you when you're quiet. Try it the next time you have a conversation with someone. Don't talk, and watch what happens. Nine times out of ten, the other person will keep talking—divulging more and more information. Don't let people know what you know, and you're certain to learn even more. Keep your plans close to the vest, and when your moment comes, *then* you flip it.

LAW 28

Be a Leader

I ain't about to feed y'all, I'm about lead y'all.
—Mike Jones, "I'm a Pimp"

THE LIFE

A pimp named Ray once posed a question to me. "Say, Pimpin', every time one of my hoes leaves, she never tells the pimp she gets with that I was her pimp," Ray said. "What's that about?"

This was my man, and I knew he had been in the game for a minute. I didn't want to burst out and say, "Nigga, you been mis-pimpin', and mis-pimpin' ain't no pimpin' at all!" Instead, I said, "Man, a ho with no instruction is bound for self-destruction. See, pimp, when you first get a ho, you have to tell that bitch the things she needs to know. After you tell her about breaking herself, the next thing you must tell her is about getting knocked—and not to reckless eyeball another pimp. And if she does decide to leave your pimpin', she must tell that other pimp to call you, to serve you. Those are the rules." Then I broke down to him why it was so important to let her know. "You tell her she must do this, because if you do see her on the track and you haven't been served the news, she's liable to get in a whole lot of shit," I told him. "But if you've been served, then you will know that she is officially with another pimp."

I explained that this also protects him, because she may not feel like going through all that and won't even bother leaving. "So the fault is not with your bitch," I told Ray. "It's your fault, because you didn't properly instruct her."

THE ISM

People think pimpin' is all about the hoes, the money, and the lifestyle. And it is. But in order to gain all of that, a pimp has to have something about himself to attract it. He has to be a leader. One thing a pimp has to understand is that it's *his* instructions that the ho is following. If a ho is out of pocket, nine times out of ten it's because of his poor-ass pimpin'. In the game they say a ho is a reflection of her pimp. So the pimp has to set proper examples to get a proper response. If you're a lazy-ass pimp who doesn't want to do shit, don't be surprised when you have some lazy-ass hoes around you. If you look like a bum and don't care about your appearance or hygiene, then your hoes will more than likely follow suit.

A lot of people put the blame on others when things don't go right, but successful leaders take the blame for the mistakes of people under them. Ultimately, if things go wrong, it's the fault of the leader, because he either didn't give good instructions or didn't get rid of the weak links in the chain.

LAW 29

Play One Ho Against the Next

They've got to compete like they're in the Kentucky Derby.
—Bishop Don Magic Juan

THE LIFE

I had these two young, fine, money-getting hoes. CeCe was my bottom bitch, but Shawn was just as valuable to me. These hoes were so fine that tricks would pay two thousand dollars just for one of them to spend the night. I was young and wanted to be the top pimp in the game, and working these two hoes—really being able to play them well—was crucial to my come-up in the game. Whenever I was alone with CeCe, I would tell her that she was the only ho that I really trusted. "One day we're going to be on top together," I told her. "You are going to be the bitch that represents me to the world." I told her that in order to get that spot, she was going to have to keep an eye on Shawn for me.

"What's up, Daddy?" she asked. "You don't trust that Shawn bitch?"

"Hell, no!" I would say. "That bitch is going to leave and choose up on another pimp one day. Fuck that bitch, and don't tell her anything we talked about, because if you do, I'm going to put her in your place. And, oh yeah, I need you to watch her. I need to know how many tricks she gets at night." CeCe would smile from ear-to-ear, just thinking that she was going to be my special private detective. What she didn't know was that Shawn had the same instructions. Man, a ho can be conniving and low down—these hoes would make up all kinds of shit to cross one another. One time Shawn told me that CeCe was fucking the tricks without a condom.

"If you're having sex with her, Daddy, be careful," she said.

She was thinking by saying that shit, I would not fuck with CeCe. But all it did was show me how the ho was hating on CeCe and wanted to take her spot. I secretly recorded our conversation, as I often did. I played it back for Cece.

"That bitch is lying, Daddy!" she said. "You know me better than that."

"Yeah, you right," I said. "But this bitch is really trying to make a move on you for that number one spot. If you want to keep my attention, get your money up, and show me *you're* the one."

Then I confronted Shawn. I told her that I shared her accusation with CeCe, and that I knew it wasn't true. I also said I understood why she told this lie—because CeCe was making more money than Shawn, so she had to cheat to stay on my good side. Shawn stuck to her story and swore that she was telling the truth. I let Shawn know that if she wanted to be down with me, she had to make that money. If she wanted to take CeCe's spot, she couldn't do it by bad-mouthing her, she had to outwork her. "Okay, bitch," I said. "Get your money right, and shit will be cool."

THE ISM

A good pimp will always use his hoes to cross one another. This is not hard to do. Every ho's ambition is to be the bottom bitch. She will lie, steal another ho's money, and even set a trap for a ho to get caught up by the police to take her spot. She will do anything to be the favored one, so it's to a pimp's advantage to play one ho against the next.

Competition breeds excellence. If you can get your workers going at one another, each trying to outdo the others, you will always win. You don't want them to be friends. You want them to distrust and dislike one another so that you end up controlling them all.

LAW 30

Prosperity over Popularity

Fuck the fame, give me the money in the game.
—Pimpin' Ken

THE LIFE

Over the years I have met a lot of former pimps who lost their minds because their money ran out before their game ran out. You can find these dudes on street corners saying, "Man, back in the day I had me a new Fleetwood with an alligator top and a Rolls Royce grill. I had a million dollars in ho money." I have even seen ex-pimps and players, who used to be the best of the best, talking to themselves on the street. They just went crazy.

One day I was riding down MLK in Milwaukee, and I saw a guy I met when I first got in the game. I said to myself, "Ain't that Fast Eddie?" I pulled over, jumped out, and said, "What's up, baby?"

He looked at me and said, "Where do I know you from?"

"Kiss my pimpin' ass, nigga!" I said. "You don't remember

me? Little Kenny Ivy? I used to pimp on that Dirty Red bitch."

"Man, I'll tell you the truth. All I can remember is all the money I fucked up," he said. "Once I got broke, my name didn't mean shit anymore. People who used to come up to me and praise me, now they cross the street when they see me coming. My family members didn't trust me around their kids, because they knew I was fucked up on drugs. When I had money, I was the shit. Young blood, I don't remember you. In fact, I don't remember nobody from back then."

"But Eddie, man, we used to pimp together," I told him. "Your bottom bitch was named Mary. She was a thieving bitch. She stole a hundred thousand dollars for you, and all the Ps were talking about that shit for years." Eddie started talking to himself. I guess thinking about that shit sent him to another place. He went from having an intelligent conversation to talking to people who weren't there.

I looked at him and said, "What can I do for you?"

"You can't do shit for me," he said. "I'm washed up. Help yourself. Save your money. You'll be okay." Then he asked me for ten dollars.

I gave him a one hundred-dollar bill and said, "Man, thanks for everything."

We said our good-byes, and as I was leaving, he said, "One more thing, Kenny. I was a bad motherfucker in my day." I nodded and kept it moving.

THE ISM

Eighty percent of the pimps, players, and hustlers that I know entered the game to be popular. Being popular isn't a bad thing, but it should be a means to some ends. My experience has taught me that you can be known by the whole world, but if you're broke, it ain't worth shit. To have a name and yet not be able to pay your bills can have a serious psychological effect on a person.

When you have money, you can buy anything, including popularity. But when you're broke, people look at you like a joke. Having popularity will not pay the bills, nor will it ensure that you eat. If you have to choose between being popular and being rich, choose the money.

LAW 31

Look Out for Suzy Choosy

All that glitters is not gold.
—Miguel de Cervantes

THE LIFE

When I first got my feet wet in the game, I saw some shit play out with a ho named Blow Job Kathy. She was on the track, choosing a new pimp every week. One day she was with Pimp Rob, the next week she was with Pimp Tommy D. I watched this ho ride the pimp merry-go-round for six months. She must have chosen fifteen pimps during this time. Each time, she broke herself for about a thousand dollars. She came with strings, too. She would only choose a pimp if he *first* let her suck his dick. She often targeted pimps who were washed up, young, or unseasoned.

One day she tried to pull this green-ass shit on my main man, Father Divine, who was very young but well-seasoned in the game. I will never forget the day Blow Job Kathy came up to Father Divine. It became legendary on the track. "Baby, I got a G for your pimpin'," Blow

Job Kathy said to him, all bold. "But the only way I will choose you is if you let me suck your dick."

Father Divine gave this ho the coldest look I had ever seen. He looked at her as if she was crazy. I thought he was going to murder that ho right there. Then out of nowhere, he broke into a smile. "You Suzy-Choosy-ass bitch!" he said. "My choosing fee is *ten thousand*. But for you, bitch, you punk-ass bitch, it's *twenty* thousand. And you got two weeks to get it up! And one more thing, bitch. Get off the pimp's dick, bitch, and get on the trick's!"

Her whole demeanor changed. She went from this bold, sassy-ass bitch to this meek, docile ho. "I . . . I already have fifteen thousand," she said, handing him her knot. "I'll have the rest for you in a week."

"Follow your money, bitch, and I'll follow you," Father Divine said.

This was real pimpin' at its finest. Word got around fast about how Father Divine flipped the script on Blow Job Kathy. A year later he finally did let Blow Job Kathy suck his dick. He said she gave some real good head, but he still preferred the bread.

THE ISM

Suzy Choosy is a very unstable ho. One minute she will, the next minute she won't. Today she's moving in this direction, tomorrow she's going in the other. This week she's with Pimpin' Paul. The next week she chooses The

Great Poke. Suzy Choosy wants to make a mockery of the pimpin'. That's her goal, and she wants to play by her own rules. A pimp thinks he's getting a prize, but soon finds out that this ho is only trying to play him and play herself. The money looks good to a pimp at first, but things that come too easily usually have a price.

What looks like a bargain may be more than you bargained for, and if something looks too good to be true, it usually is. Unreliable people don't just make themselves look bad, they make a fool out of you, too.

P
I
M
P
O
L
O
G
Y

•

LAW 32

Turn a Tramp into a Champ

I put hoes in NY onto DKNY.
—Notorious B.I.G., "Hypnotize"

THE LIFE

I have knocked many a ho because I was able to sell her on my idea of how she should look. "Say, bitch, you walking around in those Payless shoes," I would tell her. "Come fuck with this pimpin', and I'll have you in some Jimmy Choos. You need to choose a pimp who can show you how to make some real money. Tell that sucker you fucking with to get lost, and come fuck with a pimp boss. I can tell you bought that outfit at Rainbow. Let me take you to the pot of gold at the end of the rainbow."

Depending on the clientele, I would even put my hoes in business suits, with some personality glasses on—looking like sexy attorneys or schoolteachers. This always increased the tricking. A trick would see that, and his dick would get instantly hard, which meant more money for me. When I was seven deep, I called it showtime. That's when I got all my hoes together and dressed them up the way I thought they should look.

"Put on your best ho gear and your best ho face," I would tell them. "It's us against the world!"

Unfortunately, some hoes can't be helped. You just can't make them over. I had one who had a body-odor problem. I've had that problem with a few other hoes, but this one took the cake. I don't know whether she had a body-chemistry problem or what. I bought her tons of deodorant, but she was always musty. The funny thing was the ho kept making money—there must have been some desperate tricks out there, because I couldn't fuck with her. Because she was making that money, I didn't cut her for a long time. But after a while, she had to go. I told her, "Tracey, you got to go, baby. You ain't doing something right. You fucking up my business." It was a hard situation to handle, but I had to be real about it.

My other hoes said, "We're so glad you got rid of that funky bitch, Daddy." I have had hoes who didn't care about themselves, but when they fucked with me, they had to change all of that. Even if they didn't care about themselves, I cared about my money.

The Ism

Appearances are everything, and a ho has to look the part she's playing. If she comes from nothing, she has to look like something. A pimp has to polish that ho like she's a rock that he's trying to sell as a diamond. If he meets a ho from the Bronx, and she's wearing tennis shoes and some jeans, the first thing he must do is change her outfit and give her a complete makeover. His job is to make that ho more marketable, so she appeals to a trick's fantasy.

They say don't judge a book by its cover, but the truth is, that's all we do. If you have a product, people won't buy it unless the total package looks good. So much attention is paid to presentation for one purpose—if you can appeal to a customer's fantasies, he will buy what you're selling.

LAW 33

Bring Your People with You to the Top

If you eat good, everyone around you should.
—Eduard Davis

THE LIFE

I have been in nightclubs and seen these so-called ballers walk in with their entourages. These suckers will have on about one hundred thousand dollars in jewels, they will buy out the bar, and if they're feeling really good, they will throw a few hundred dollars into the crowd. All of this is to make them look good, like a star, but their boys look like shit—no money, no fresh clothes, no jewels, just looking fucked up. Then this man is wondering why his boys are hating on him. He will think it's jealousy, but it's not. They are saying to themselves, "This motherfucker wants us hanging around him, but he's not sharing the wealth. Fuck him!" This dude didn't look out for everyone, and he should have.

Back in the day, when I was hanging with my man, Frog, if he stole anything, he would make sure that I had first action at that shit. If I had something, I would share it with Frog, JD, and whoever else was down with us. When I started doing movies, I made sure to put them down and gave them parts in my movie. My main man, Eduard Davis, told me when I did my first movie to make sure to hook up people like White Folks, Scorpio, Gorgeous Dre, and all of those other pimps. He told me I should make sure they came up too. He was right, because ultimately, by elevating them, it made me look even bigger. I wouldn't be where I am today if someone didn't look out for me. So if I eat, everybody around me eats.

When I came home from the joint, JD—who gave me my first ho and started me off in the game—gave me some thousands to get back on my feet. That's what you do, especially if you have it, because stuff like that always has a way of coming back full circle. In our twenty-seven years of knowing each other, JD and I have benefited greatly from taking care of each other. In late 2006 I was able to put JD up on a lick to buy himself a brand new S 55 Benz, which looked good as hell, and it felt great to see him in it.

The Ism

The first thing people say when they get on top is, "I'm going to bring my guys with me." Some do, but most don't. Most people only look out for themselves, and while that may seem cool, it can also be your undoing. In the game people have individuals around them who would rob them, who would kill them, who would set them up to go to jail, or who would try to fuck up their reputation. A lot of the motivation behind this activity may be jealousy, but another part can simply be a feeling of a lack of appreciation. Money and success attract people, but the worst thing in the world is to have a bunch of people around you, and yet none of them are really down with you.

Just like misery loves company, so does prosperity. How much fun can you have at the top, if you have no one there to share it all with? If you make it big, take care of those who helped you get there. If you have a chance to become a millionaire, why not make sure that your friends have the same chance? Hell, if everyone around you has their own shit, there's less of a chance that they will be borrowing from you. It's not enough to just give people things. That's not what I'm talking about. The best gifts aren't handed to people, but are shown to people, so they can work for themselves. There's an expression: Give a man a fish, and he eats for a day; teach a man to fish, and he eats for the rest of his life. For all that the game has given me, this book is my way of giving back.

LAW 34

Show Respect to Get Respect

Nigga respect the game, that should be it, what you eat don't make me shit. —Jay Z, "Heart of the City"

They call me the Godfather of the Game, even the police respect me. —Fillmore Slim

THE LIFE

When I was young, one of the things the old players used to say is, "Boy, respect your elders." I always obeyed this law, but one day it came into question. I was in my after-hours spot in Milwaukee on the east side, and this older pimp associate of mine was in there drunk and acting way out of pimp mode. "Young punk, you ain't no pimp," he said to me. "I heard all your bitches are on your payroll!" This was a real insult, because what he was saying was that I was paying my hoes, which is a no-no. Now I'm not going to lie, this was one of the most confusing incidents of my career. I was taught never to disrespect the OGs, but this washed-up player was out of bounds.

"Say, man, you are going from a pimp-aholic to an alcoholic," I said. "I know they say the liquor is quicker, and you may be looking for a fast ride to the senior citizen home, but you need to get a hammer, and hit your pimpin' in the head until your pimpin' falls dead, old-ass nigga! You ain't heard shit because your old ass is game-impaired. And for the record, Hank Aaron—era ass nigga, if I pay a ho, it's with the money I just checked from that ho!"

At this point my man Pimpin' Poke jumped in. "Young pimp, you're wrong for disrespecting this veteran pimp like that," he said to me. "Take it easy, Greasy." I looked at Pimpin' Poke, because I couldn't believe what he was saying. Did he just miss the whole scene? Before I could open my mouth, OG put his foot in his mouth again.

"We don't need no referee!" he said.

Poke looked at this lost case. "Man, what's the matter? You ain't got no treads left on those Goodyear tires?"

"Yeah, man," I said. "Back then was a hen, and useta was a motherfucking rooster. If he don't get with the here and now, I'm going to take his shine and shit on this old-ass nigga with this young-ass pimpin'."

Years later, when I became a veteran pimp, I had a few young boys try their hands at disrespecting me. I knew they were the Pepsi generation, but they couldn't fuck with a Coke Classic. One day I was on the track with my man JD, and this upstart fresh sucker tried to challenge me. He pulled up in his new S 600 Benz, looking real fly. "Who's the most pimpin'-est nigga on the track?" he boldly asked.

"Why you want to know?" JD popped back.

"I'm looking to knock him for every bitch he has!" this sucker said.

"Ain't nothing but veteran pimps here, homie." JD was trying to warn him. "What are you saying?"

"All I can say is that there is big pimpin' in town, and I'm coming for the motherfucking crown!" I was quiet, just watching this dude with his chest puffed out, but when he said that wild shit, I looked at JD and winked. It was a signal that it was time to coon this motherfucker. Cooning was a common practice among veteran pimps, where they worked together to teach a disrespectful motherfucker a lesson.

The plan was for JD to pretend to be cool with this dude, so he would be able to get me a rundown of all of his hoes. I told him, "I want you to tell me how many hoes this buster has, and if you can, see if he will give you any information on those hoes."

By the time I was ready for my first mission, JD had found out which ho would be easiest to knock. I rolled up on this ho on the track and started sweating her. Thanks to JD, I knew her name, where she was from, and I was even able to tell her that she got her ass beaten two days before. The ho chose up, because she knew her nigga was slippin'.

Once I got inside his household with the first ho, the rest was easy. I asked her which of the remaining two was the weaker one. "Brittany, the tall blonde," she told me. I asked her who was Brittany's favorite artist, and she told me it was Tupac. For three days straight I drove up to her on the track, blasting "Me Against the World" and "All

Eyez on Me" with my windows down. Finally, after the third day, the ho spoke.

"How do you know I like Tupac, with your fine ass?" she asked.

"Bitch, get in!" I said. "I'm tired of being your deejay. It's time for me to be your pimp." Two down, one more to go.

After I served this young pimp for two bitches, he'd had enough. He was out of town before sundown, but I still wasn't satisfied. I wasn't done making him pay for his disrespect. I had JD call old boy and find out where he was with his third ho. I found out that he was in Las Vegas. I packed up my most trusted ho and sent her on a plane to Vegas with specific instructions.

She caught up with dude's ho at Caesar's. My ho told her how pretty she was, how she was looking for a new daddy, and that she wanted to choose her fine-ass man. The other ho didn't have a clue that she was being set up. For two weeks my ho worked her way into old boy's stable. She got real close with his ho, flipped her, bought her a plane ticket, and had her on the next thing smoking back to Milwaukee.

As is customary, when I had the ho in my possession, I called dude to serve him the news. "Nigga, don't you ever try to outshine a vet!" I told him. "What you need to do is go back to your past and let this pimpin' kick you in your ass."

THE ISM

If a pimp keeps it one hundred percent at all times and shows love for the game, he has my utmost respect. If he disrespects this game, I don't care how much of an OG he is—I don't have any respect for a lame. But if you can, you should try to give respect even when you feel it's undeserved, because it can go a long way. No one wants to be shown up; it's embarrassing and humiliating, and they *will* seek revenge. The best rule of thumb is to treat people the way you want to be treated, at least to their faces.

Law 35

Trust Nothing but the Game

Where large sums of money are concerned, it is advisable to trust nobody. —Agatha Christie

My money's my honey . . . 'In God We Trust' tatted on her tummy. —Chamillionaire, "Me & My Money"

THE LIFE

I had this discussion with my man Jay, who I had known for years. He always kept it real with me. He told me that he had a girl, but he was fucking her sister whenever his girl went to work. "Why would you fuck your girl's sister?" I asked him.

"The bitch trusts me like a motherfucker," he said.

"How does her sister feel about that?"

"Her sister has been fucking all of her men for the last ten years," he told me.

"That's a nasty bitch!" I said. "Give me her number." He gave it to me, I spit some game, and she was down with me. I never trusted her, though, and for good reason. One day I was having a barbeque at my house, and my homie came by. We were really close. I was outside with everybody, and I noticed that the ho was nowhere in sight. I didn't care where she was, as long as she was getting some paper. Then I noticed that my friend was gone too, and I finally had to investigate. I found that ho in my house fucking my homie—for *free*! Now, I knew she was capable of anything, but my friend was my main man. I checked both of them and made them get the fuck out of my house.

This gave me a new perspective, and I changed my style a bit. No nigga was allowed to speak to my hoes, and my hoes weren't allowed to look at anyone, unless it was about some paper. My distrust started to spread. When I was just hanging out, I kept my guard up, and I only gave up information on a need-to-know basis. I could be in a town for years, and niggas wouldn't even know I was there. When a young brother came to me for some game, I would feed him some bullshit, because I didn't trust anyone. I thought everyone would just use whatever game I gave them against me. After my own homeboy pulled that bullshit, I wasn't giving anyone an opportunity to take anything from me again. I would test the people around me—my hoes and my homies—by leaving money in certain places around certain people, to see if they would steal it. One time I left a large sum in my truck to test a certain person (you know who you are). They failed with flying colors, but I never said a word. This was someone I thought I could trust, but I had learned that you can't trust anyone in this game.

The Ism

There is not a person on this Earth over the age of eighteen who has not been crossed by someone they trusted. This was more than likely a person they shared everything with, because it's usually the people closest to you who have the ability to hurt you the most. Believe it or not, even your family could be the ones to take you out. They know the most, and as we say in this game, knowledge is power. That power can work against you, too.

Money doesn't know love. When you're doing business, it's best to put nothing by anyone. People are funny when it comes to money, and trust is a commodity that you just can't afford.

LAW 36

Be Internationally Known, Nationally Recognized, and Locally Accepted

From Frisco to Maine and all the way to Spain. —R.P.

THE LIFE

As a young man, I thought I was doing the damn thing, but the old local heads were still constantly grooming me. They knew that eventually I would have to get out of town and really put it down.

About fifteen years ago I was in the local after-hours club. A bunch of us were sitting at a table shooting the shit. One veteran pimp, Tommy Dixon, was roasting a young up-and-coming pimp named JB. He was a live nigga with about five Cadillacs and seven hoes. He was always jacking about his success as a pimp. Tommy interrupted JB and said, "Boy, you're crazy if you think I'm going to respect your local pimpin'. Nigga, I done pimped all over the world and have a ho in Japan right now, getting my dough!"

All JB could say was, "Man, my hoes give me my money right here in Milwaukee just the same."

I was sharp enough as a young pimp to know how the

old vets were. I would be next, so I acted like I was going to get me a drink. But Tommy peeped me. "Young pimp, where are you going?" he said, stopping me in my tracks.

I had to think quickly. "Nigga, I'm going to the phone to tell my bitch in New York to get to a Western Union and wire me that ho money she's been stacking," I said boldly. Old Tommy looked at me like he wanted to whoop my young ass, but one thing he knew—just like I couldn't prove he didn't have a ho in Japan, he couldn't prove that I *didn't* have a ho in New York.

From that time I have been just about everywhere in the world. I basically lived on the road. I went to fifty states and put it down. Looking back, I can truly say that hitting the road was one of the best things that ever happened to me, because I had the chance to meet all types of people. When I was in Los Angeles, I met a guy named Dooley. We were at a movie set doing a film with rapper Mack 10. Dooley was a boss player, and he had an after-hours spot on Crenshaw.

"I heard a lot about you," Dooley said. "And from what I heard, you're a nice pimp."

"Yeah, it depends on who you talk to," I said. "I'm okay."

"I see you be in L.A. a lot," he said. "Why don't you come on down to my after-hours spot when you get off the set?"

"Shiiit," I said. "I'm finished now. Let's go!"

When we got to the joint, I was there for twenty

minutes when Chaka Khan and the rapper Dru Down walked in. They both came over and spoke to me, and that really impressed Dooley. I wished old Tommy Dixon could have seen me then. I'd have said to him, "Things done changed since back in the day. I stay in pimp mode, and I've got fifty-two zip codes!"

THE ISM

Had I stayed only in Milwaukee, there would never be a Pimpin' Ken. I think back to those old pimps, and I wonder if they ever knew what it's like to be written about in French, Japanese, Spanish, and Yoruba.

When you're local, the game goes in a circle, and everybody knows the same shit. If people see your ass everyday, you get too familiar, and the things you do don't seem special. You can't have a victorious homecoming if you never left in the first place.

LAW 37

Let a Ho Know

It ain't matrimony, it's macaroni!
—Kenny Red

THE LIFE

About nine years ago I was at Magic City, a famous strip club in Atlanta. A stripper asked me, "Do you want a dance?"

"What did you say? Am I from France?"

"No, do you want a dance?"

"Yeah," I said. "Put that money in my pants."

"You're a pimp, ain't you?" she asked.

"You're a ho, ain't you?" I shot back.

"Hell no!" she said, indignant. "I'm an *entertainer*."

"Okay, ho," I said. "Well, go entertain then."

"Why'd you ask me if I was a ho?"

"Because you *are* a ho," I told her. "You're on the low end of ho'ing, tippy-toeing. And for dollar tips, which ain't shit."

"Okay, your hoes sell pussy and make more money,"

she said. "But what are those hoes going to do if they catch AIDS?"

"You talking about germs and diseases, but you walking around here with no clothes on?" I said. "Real hoes practice safe sex and get it in advance. It's bitches like you who take a chance."

As she walked away, she bent over. "Don't you want some of this good pussy?" she asked.

"Yeah, bitch. To sell!" She laughed, and then she went around and told the whole club that I was a pimp. For the rest of the night those strippers knew to keep their distance unless they had some assistance. One came up to me just before the club closed. She asked me for a tip.

I said, "If I tip you, I have to pimp you!"

She got mad and said, "You can't pay a bitch?"

"Bitch, I am paying you. I'm *paying* you no attention!"

"Well, can't you buy a bitch a drink?"

"Sure, bitch," I said. "With *your* money."

She finally left, but after she got dressed, she came back and said, "I like your style. What does a bitch have to do to get with your pimpin'?"

"Sock it to my pocket like a rocket!"

She reached in her purse, pulled out eight hundred dollars, and said, "I choose, but only because you didn't try to play me."

THE ISM

When a ho comes up to a man, she's trying to get him to spend some money. A pimp has to let her know from the door that it's not going to be a party like that with him. If she's fucking with him, she's the one who will have to pay. If he doesn't let her know, she will be coming at him like she would a trick. If she does know and yet she's still in a pimp's face, then they both know he's about to add another ho to his stable.

Be up front about who you are and what your intentions are. If your targets stay, they are yours. If they don't, they weren't ever going to be.

P
I
M
P
O
L
O
G
Y

•

LAW 38

Wreck a Hater

Never interrupt your enemy when
he is making a mistake. —John Milton

It's a cold world, so homie bundle up.
—Lil' Wayne, "Hustler Musik"

THE LIFE

A few years back there was this certain individual who was really shitting on my game. He was trying hard to destroy me. At this time I was on all kinds of albums and I had a few movies on the market, so people wanted to hear what this guy was saying. The first thing I did was keep my mouth shut so that he wouldn't gain any momentum.

I went and found everyone who knew this nigga and asked them what they knew about him. Once I got my ammunition, I stepped to this nigga and asked him politely to stop shitting on my name. He tried to diss me in front of some big pimps. I could tell from their faces that they were taking sides. But this, too, was part of my plan. I wanted him to look like he was a big-old pimp. I wanted all of those suckers who believed the shit he was spreading to get caught up too. I walked away, looking like I was defeated. After I left, he said, "See, I told you that nigga Ken is a buster." I know this because I had spies in that crowd.

Someone else said, "Yeah, the man didn't even try to defend his rep!" What they didn't know was that I was building his confidence to keep talking shit, so when I did bring his monkey-ass down, *all* the niggas who were on his dick would feel like fools. They would feel like they had been played by him, and after that they wouldn't fuck with him ever again.

I called a good friend of mine who the nigga thought was cool with him. I invited this mark and a few other top players to a Super Bowl party at this major club. I knew my friend would bring that simp, too. I waited for just about every pimp in the country to show up before I let his ass have it. I waited until the appointed time, when I had everyone's attention. I reminded all of the guys who I had known for years that this buster was new on the scene. He only had five years in the game. I told them that he got into the game by giving all the leaking, broke pimps money to speak highly of him. That's how he got his reputation—he paid for it.

A few of them nodded as they listened, but I wasn't finished. Then I hit them with the big revelation. "This nigga is an FBI informant!" I said. "He's a motherfucking snitch!"

The whole crowd looked at him and said, "Pimp, is that truth?"

He was stunned. He had no idea that I had this information, and he couldn't say shit. One thing about the game, if people find out something about you that you had been hiding, then they will think that *everything* you've said to them has been a lie. In the case of this motherfucker, all of those pimps who were hanging out with him all of sudden started worrying about what they had said to this nigga that could get them locked up.

I caught everyone off-guard. Everyone was fucked up now, and that pimp's career was officially over. He was done. And, more important, everybody knew not to fuck with Ken.

THE ISM

You'll meet people who just don't like you, and they'll do whatever they can to stop your groove. In the streets you can handle the problem in many different ways. You can shoot the motherfucker and spend the rest of your life in jail—or maybe someone who knew him will come back and kill you. I never use violence, because pimpin' is a mind game for me. I may destroy someone, but he'll be okay. He just won't have a career when I'm through. I try my best to put that person out of commission or do them so bad that they don't want any more. As I've always said, "All's fair in love, war, and pimpin'." It's a cold game, but it's a fair game.

If someone is throwing dirt at you, find out as much dirt on them as you can and bury them in it. Keeping your mouth closed is a good starting tactic, because it makes the other person seem like he is babbling, like he's just hating on you. Then you need spies in the game who stay up on the haters and keep you posted on what's being said. If your spies dig deep enough, they can find things in anyone's past that they don't want known. Once you have this information, you shut your enemies down—but make sure that they never see it coming.

LAW 39

Switch Up

*It is not the strongest of the species that survive,
nor the most intelligent, but the one most responsive to change.*
—Charles Darwin

*And if I flop I switch the hustle, I learn the game
and then set up shop.* —Paul Wall, "Ridin' Dirty"

THE LIFE

My daddy was the master of reinventing himself. In the
same day he would be in the street breaking niggas all after-
noon and then come home and be a father, taking us to the
movies and spending time with my mother. He would go as
far as to work square construction jobs. By the time I was
fourteen, I was able to understand how my pops could take
a break from the street life and chill. One day I asked him
what was really going on. Why was he going through all
these changes?

"The streets are like the jungle," he said. "Sometimes
you have to be the lion and attack the prey, but sometimes
you have to camouflage to survive. One day they may see
me in a suit, the next day they see me with a construction
hat," he told me. "This is why they call me Johnny Slick,
because they can't peep my game."

All through my pimp career, I was a very flashy dresser.

After I did *Pimps Up, Ho's Down*, I became a filmmaker. I reinvented my style, and this turned the pimp world upside down and kept them talking about Pimpin' Ken.

THE ISM

Any pimp who doesn't switch up will lose his hoes. Hoes are funny—once they get used to you, learn your game, and get comfortable, they don't respond the same way. A pimp must switch his jewels, cars, minks, and style every now and then. He has to keep a ho on her toes by staying on his. He has to turn that 500 Benz into a 600 Benz, that mink jacket into a full-length chinchilla, that three-carat diamond pinky ring into a five-carat.

If you don't get brand new, people will think you fell off. Anyone who stays the same is in a rut, and you have to make changes to stay ahead of the game. You have to keep people wondering what you're going to come up with next.

LAW 40

Don't Down 'Em, Crown 'Em

There is no such thing as bad publicity,
except your own obituary. —Brendan Behan

When someone says 'Rosebudd's a motherfucker,'
that's the highest compliment you can get, because
they've run out of adjectives. —Rosebudd

THE LIFE

My man Aquarius always had something bad to say about the other pimps. If I said something like, "That dude is a real pimp! He's got a new Benz and three hoes." Aquarius would say, "Man, that nigga sells dope on the side. He ain't no pimp!"

If I said, "I just kicked it with Pimpin' L.B. and he gave me some real game," Aquarius would say, "Fuck, dude! He can't even keep a ho. How's he going to *teach* on a ho?" Aquarius was a hater. There was always some hate shit going on with him. The funny thing was, the other pimps were no better. Everyone was hating on everyone else.

I knew that as long as I stayed on top, the pimps would always try to put my pimpin' down. Pimps would tell their hoes that I was a drug dealer, and that I made deals with hoes, so I would look like a fake pimp. The thing they didn't know was that the more they hated on me, the more a ho wanted to see for herself if what they said was true.

One day in the club this one ho saw me and kept looking. Finally, I went up to her and ran a usual line: "Damn, baby, you're so fine, your mama should have had triplets!"

"If she did, what would you have done with us?" she said.

"I would be three deep and put all you bitches down," I told her.

"Hold up!" she said. "Are you trying to say you're a pimp now?" Apparently, she had heard something different about me from her pimp.

"Listen, you out-of-pocket bitch. I was born a pimp!" I told her. "I ought to put a charge on your ass for talking to me this long."

"Sir, I think you're a very sexy man and one of the best dressers in town," she said. "But all your friends said you are not a pimp. That's why I wanted to see about you for myself."

"Bitch, if I'm so handsome, pay my ransom!"

"What's your choosing fee?" she asked. With that, she chose up and broke herself, and I had to serve her former pimp the news that blew his fuse.

The Ism

Hating is so much a part of the game that long after I got out, people were *still* hating on me. The more they hate, the more people want to know if what is being said is true.

It keeps them interested. Thank God for the haters. If they didn't hate, no one would care who Pimpin' Ken is—but that didn't mean I was going to return the favor.

If people are hating on you, it means you must be doing something right. The only time people have something to say about you is if you're doing big things, if you're a somebody. The more people talk about you—good or bad—the more people want to know about you. When you hate on others, you make them the star on stage, while you're just a critic in the audience.

LAW 41

Keep Your Front Up Till You Come Up

We going to keep our spirits up, and that's going to make us winners right there. —Scorpio

THE LIFE

Years ago I was in Vegas, and I had four hoes with me. We were getting plenty of money, but I had a very bad gambling problem. Vegas was the worst place I could be. I couldn't seem to win for nothing. For three months I was getting my ass handed to me at the blackjack and roulette tables. Somehow, I was smart enough not to spend the money we needed to live on. I always took care of the basics, but had nothing left for flossing and treating my hoes to shopping sprees, which would be my norm. I don't know how I kept them in the dark for so long, but one thing I can tell you, I dressed up every night and talked cash money shit.

"You hoes are making so much money, I paid a Brinks truck five hundred dollars just to take our money back to Milwaukee," I told them. I had to come up with a story to explain why the money in Vegas was so short. "So you hoes get ready, 'cause we're going shopping for a whole week when we get back to Milwaukee!" Finally, my luck at the tables changed, and I started winning. I was able to make back much of what I had lost, so I really could take them shopping when we got back.

Even at my lowest, I would put on my mink, gators, and jewels, get in my freshest whip, and parade around. In my mind, if I looked like the perfect pimp, a ho would stay choosing. There have been many times when things weren't right, but I kept myself up until I was able to come up.

THE ISM

The one thing a ho won't tolerate is a pimp fucking up the money. They never want to feel like they are ho'ing for nothing or to support a drug or gambling habit. If he looks weak to her, she will choose another pimp. So he must always keep up his front. Most players in the game are good at fooling people—looking like they got it going on. They make themselves seem like they're more than they are. Every lady has seen that brother in the club, with a tight fit on, big gold chain, nice watch, looking real slick with a hot whip, only to find out later that he lives with his mama. Every fella has met that fine chick in the club—the one with the big ass, the Fendi bag, the nice hairdo, but once he got to her crib, she has eight kids, and the house is a mess.

Everything that glitters ain't gold, but if you appear perfect, you will more than likely be seen that way. How people first see you is how they will judge you, so you must make sure that they see you at your very best—or pretending to be your best. My man Michael Maroy used to always say, "If people think you're flawed like them, they will try to prove that they are better than you." That's an opportunity you don't want to give them.

LAW 42

If You Can See It, You Can Be It

Whatever the mind of man can conceive and believe,
it can achieve. —Napoleon Hill

THE LIFE

When I was in the game, I used to lock myself in a hotel
room far away from my hoes and the track. I would
meditate on the situation I was in and envision where I
wanted to be. I would try to see all of the players in the
game in my mind—the cars they drove, the jewels they
wore, how they looked, and how many hoes each of them
had. I saw them, and then I saw myself with all of it. In
my head I would create different imaginary scenarios of
how I wanted it to go down. I saw exactly how I would
play them out.

I knew for it all to work, I had to have perfect timing.
To have perfect timing, you have to have everything
sorted out *before* it goes down. Only once I finished putting my thoughts together did I go to the streets and
make my moves.

The Ism

Pimpin' is about controlling minds, and you have to learn to control your own before you can control someone else's. Every action starts with a thought. Before a general puts a battle plan into action, he thinks it through first. He visualizes the strategy, then he puts it in motion. By the time the conflict begins, it doesn't really matter if he goes out on the battlefield or not. It was won or lost before it began—in his mind.

Wise men know that in order to be ahead of a situation, you must first see that situation in your head. If you're going to be somewhere at a certain time, before you even get to that place, your mind has an image of where you're going. You can picture the place, the buildings, the people, everything. Then you can map out your course, write down your plan, and make a move.

LAW 43

Talk Shit and Swallow Spit

You ain't from Russia, so bitch why you Russian?
—Nelly, "Pimp Juice"

*I got more game than the Parker Brothers and more flavor than
a Now 'n' Later. Let me reach out and touch you, like AT&T,
and bring good things to life, like GE.* —Pimpin' Ken

THE LIFE

I was at a Tyson fight in Las Vegas in 1996. He was fighting
for the heavyweight championship against Frank Bruno, and
I was there profiling with my hoes. On our way into the
arena we bumped into Don King. Don King is one of the
men I had admired from afar over the years, and here I was
face-to-face with him. So I said to him, "Man, you are one of
the few people who talks more shit than I do. Did you go to
school for all of that shit you be talking?"

He smiled and said, "Why should I go to school to
matriculate, when I'm earning without the learning?"

That seemed to tickle the shit out of my hoes, who burst
out laughing. I turned to them and said, "You hoes are out of
pocket, be cool!" They were showing me up, and I had to
recover. "Sir," I said to Don King, "I have a Ph.D."

"In what?" he asked.

"A pimpin' hoes degree!" I said. He slapped me five and

walked away, smiling from ear-to-ear. Holding my own with a legend made me feel like a million, and it reminded my hoes why it was *me* they were ho'ing for.

THE ISM

Most of the pimps who got knocked for their hoes, got knocked by a slick-talking nigga like me—pimps with diarrhea of the mouth, who talk more shit than a fat bitch's toilet. In order for a ho to look up to you, you must have something for a ho to look up to. No ho will follow a pimp who doesn't have a winning personality—at least not for long.

Conversation rules the nation. All great leaders are good orators. For years I studied the great leaders and incorporated their shit into my game. Those on top have the gift of gab—they know how to sell it. If you ever want to reach the highest heights, you'll have to develop this quality in yourself.

LAW 44

You Need Fire and Desire

Goals are not only absolutely necessary to motivate us.
They are essential to really keep us alive. —Robert H. Schuller

She fuck wit me because I got big dreams.
—T.I., "What's Yo Name?"

THE LIFE

When I was a young man, I was always getting in trouble.
One day that trouble caught up with me, and I had to go do
some time in the joint. At this time I had no plan. All I
knew was that I wanted to be rich, and that's what landed
me in jail.

While I was in the joint, this OG named Art asked me
some questions about setting goals. "What's your desire in
life?" he asked me. I had never even thought about what
desire really meant, let alone what I desired in life. I was so
confused that I made up a lie on the spot. I told him I had to
do something and that I'd be right back. I excused myself,
went to the prison library, and asked the librarian if she had
any books on goals and desire. She pointed to the left and
said, "Those are the self-help books over there."

I went to the self-help section and the first book I saw
was Dale Carnegie's *How to Win Friends and Influence*

People. I thought I could breeze right through it. I would skim it and get back to old dude with a great answer. Well, that was almost twenty-two years ago, and I haven't stopped reading that book. I find myself referring back to it to this day.

When I came home, I told myself that as soon as I hit the bricks, I was going to get on my feet. Since then I've had quite a few bumps on this road. There were times when it seemed like I wasn't going to make it. One day I'd have cash; the next day I was broke. One day everybody loved me; the next day everybody hated me. But through it all I kept my head up, and I had a burning desire to win. I look at how my life used to be, and I think, "I'm doing mighty damn good now!"

THE ISM

As I reflect on the many great men and women who have walked this Earth, one thing they all had was a burning desire to be great. Anything you do in life begins with a desire. Someone who wants to be the best has to have a desire so strong that it can't be stopped. Desire keeps your goals moving down the road to success.

LAW 45

Get Rid of the Word "If"

Remember that if ifs *and* ands *were pots and pans,*
the whole world would be a kitchen. —Pimpin' Ken

THE LIFE

Napoleon Hill's *Think and Grow Rich* had an impact on
my life and how I approached the game. Hill has a chap-
ter devoted to this word "if" and how it stops people
from accomplishing all that they could. People have so
many "if onlys" that they believe, which have kept them
from being all they could be. Here is the kind of shit I
hear all the time:

- IF I HAD MORE MONEY ...
- IF I HAD A BETTER EDUCATION ...
- IF I DIDN'T HAVE DEBT ...
- IF I HAD ME A WHITE GIRL ...
- IF I DIDN'T HAVE A CRIMINAL RECORD ...
- IF I HAD DR. DRE PRODUCING MY ALBUM ...
- IF I HAD A BETTER ENVIRONMENT ...
- IF I HAD AS MUCH GAME AS PIMPIN' KEN ...

These are the thoughts of people who fail. We have to get rid of the alibis and the excuses. My man, Jim Brown, said that you have to change that "I can't" mentality into an "I can" mentality. I learned a long time ago that you can talk yourself out of things, and you can talk your way into things. I believe there is nothing I can't do or have, and because I believe that, there *is* nothing I can't do or have. That works the same in the negative. If you always set yourself up by talking about what you can't do, or if you only had a little more of this you could do more, then you will continue to fail.

THE ISM

The reason we have a hard time succeeding is because of the alibis we use. If you're somebody working to get out of the excuse-making mentality, make sure you stay around people with a similar mind-set. When you see a person making excuses about everything, you need to run for the door, because that person is a dream-killer.

LAW 46

Move and Shake Like a Pimp Shakes

A pimp's not gonna starve for nothing, a pimp is gonna get it.
—Pimpin' Snooky

THE LIFE

I would tell all my hoes, "If I have to tell you to get up and go to work, this game is not for you. You have to make it your business to get up every day and get that long green."

This one ho didn't get it. "Daddy, why we can't wait for you to give us instruction to go to work?" she asked me.

"Bitch, *these* are my instructions: Get off your ass, and get some money! Look, before you got in the game, what did you do?" I asked her.

"I used to be a cleaning woman at a hotel," she told me.

"Well, what happened?"

"They got mad because I wouldn't do any extra work," she said. "I told them, I was only going to do what I got paid for."

"Bitch, there is your problem. All you had to do was go the extra mile, and you would have become the boss," I told her. "That attitude is the same reason why you aren't my bottom bitch. I shouldn't have to *tell* you what to do. You should have the personal initiative to get it on your own."

Then she hit me with another question: "Do I give the trick more than what he pays for?"

"No, the trick only gets what he pays for," I said. "When you're on the track, you're the boss. You're the one in control. The trick kisses your ass—not the other way around."

When I first got into the entertainment business, I tried to do it like the big boys. I hired a street team, spent a lot of money on marketing, started the website www.pimpinken.net, worked closely with my publicist, and sat back, expecting everyone to do the job I had paid them to do. After six months I peeped that if I was going to take it to the next level, I had to get on my grind, roll up my sleeves, and get to work. I woke up one day and said, "I've got this movie, *Pimpology Uncut*, and this shit has to get to the streets." I didn't wait for anyone to do what I had to do—I traveled all over the United States, selling that tape myself out of the trunk of my car.

THE ISM

People think they're cheating their bosses when they do the bare minimum on their job, but they're really only cheating themselves. They are sitting back waiting for someone to tell them what to do, thinking they doing their jobs, but that will keep them at the bottom. When bosses see you taking the initiative, they know they are getting more than what they're paying for, and they like that. Then they know you are worthy of a promotion.

Most people want other people to do things for them, or they are so lazy that they'll wait until it's too late to do anything. When you want something to happen, you have to make it happen. Shit won't happen just because you're sitting around wishing that it would happen. You have to take the first step.

LAW 47

Pimpin' Is What You Do, Not Who You Are

Before you are a pimp, you've got to be a man.
—Gorgeous Dre

THE LIFE

A young pimp by the name of Ivory P once asked me, "Are we just pimps and that's all?"

"Why'd you ask me a question like that?" I asked him. "You don't know who the fuck you are?"

"Nah, pimp. It's ain't like that. But I hear a lot of veteran pimps say, 'I pimp and that's all I want to do. I'm going to pimp or die!'"

"Yeah, no disrespect to the vets," I told him. "But pimpin' is what I do, it's not who I am. When I go to my mother's house, I'm her son, Ken Ivy. When I'm with my sons, Little Kenny and Supreme, I'm Daddy."

I was at my mom's house one day, and she had some company over. One of the ladies had the nerve to say, "I've seen your son on TV. Ain't he a big-time pimp?"

My mother smiled. "Let me tell you something, honey," my mama said. "That's my baby. He ain't no pimp.

He's just a big-headed boy whose diapers I used to change ten times a day." Listening to my mother made me realize that we are different to different people. The things we do in one area of our daily activities have nothing to do with who we are in other areas. Here I was, one of the top players in the game, and mama is telling people how I used to shit in my drawers. All the years I spent in the game didn't mean a thing to her. To my mama, I was still just that big-headed boy.

My daddy used to go around to the real street players and say, "You know Pimpin' Ken? That's my son, and he knows who's the boss. I used to whoop his ass." He was proud of me, but he also wanted to let people know that he was the boss. I was able to relate to that when I had my kids. No matter how big they get, you're always the daddy.

I always know who I am and what hat I'm wearing, depending on the circumstances, but sometimes it's other people who get confused. There are people who don't want to do legitimate business with me, because they think I forced women to sell their bodies—but how do you force the willing? On the other hand, try not paying your taxes, and see how fast the government forces their pimp hand on you. When I do business, I occasionally hear people say, "You're not going to pimp me!" Now how dumb is that, unless you're going to break yourself? When I am at the table doing business, I am no more a pimp than any other businessman. If you're at the business table and you aren't on your game, you will be pimped by someone. It's up to you to figure out the game, not to worry about someone else's past hustle—or ignore all the "legitimate" hustles going on right under your nose.

THE ISM

Real pimpin', you will never see coming. It will hit your ass so hard, you may find yourself supporting a war, and you don't even know why. Real pimpin' is so powerful that you will allow a president to take office when he doesn't win the popular vote. It's so real that a vice president can shoot a man with the reckless use of a weapon, and nothing happens to him. The man he shot will end up apologizing to the public, while the average young brother on the street will serve twenty-five-to-life for attempted murder. And you call *me* a pimp?

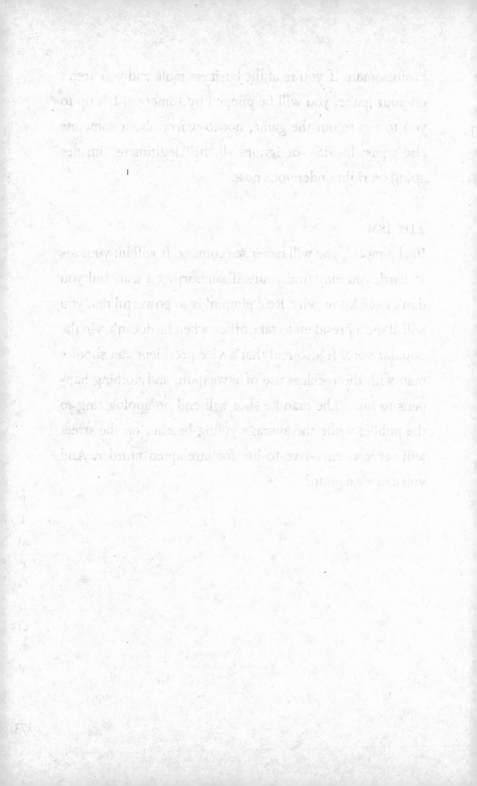

LAW 48

Don't Believe the Hype

Knowledge is power. —Sir Francis Bacon

THE LIFE

The older I got, the sharper I thought I was getting. But as my man Big Phil used to say to me, "You're getting duller." You tend to get slower and you slip more, the longer you stay in the game. Your game gets tired. That's why I knew that I always had to have my exit plan ready to go.

If you think you're going to take the information in this book and be the next Pimpin' Ken, think again. Pimpin' hoes like we did back in the day is really a thing of the past. The so-called pimp game that's being played today ain't shit compared to the way it used to be. I haven't pimped on hoes for a while. I'm not showing any disrespect to those who still are doing that, but if you can't figure out how to flip the script and pimp on something that can really make you rich, something that is legal and can make sure that you never have to work again, then you shouldn't really call yourself a pimp.

The truth is that most people in this game end up in prison, on drugs, or dead. There are very few past the age of forty who are alive and successful. I tested this theory by calling around the country, checking on some of the real players and ballers who were around when I was in the game. I would ask about Pimpin' L.B.—who was seven deep with all of the cars and jewels in the world.

"Oh, he has AIDS," someone told me. "Full-blown, not doing too well."

A lot of pimps, while preaching the use of condoms, take risks with their lives every day with those hoes. But even with condoms, they do break, and there you go. A lot of pimps also meet their maker when a ho's family member finds out about her ho'ing. A big brother who may have just gotten out of jail to find his sister out there ho'ing will be looking for that pimp. And when he finds the pimp—that's his ass. I know so many pimps who have been killed by angry family members who blame the pimp for that ho's life choice. More and more pimps are being sent to jail for everything from tax evasion to statutory rape. Law enforcement is trying to really crack down on the oldest profession in the world—at least on the management side of things. Pimpin' ain't easy.

I was blessed—not lucky, because there's no such thing as luck. I knew that I was put here for something more, or at least that's what my mama always told me. So, do know that my goal is to teach the wisdom of the pimp mentality, not how to become a peddler of flesh. As long as you stay on that low-level pimpin', you can never be a threat, make a difference, or do something great.

THE ISM

The value of this game is in learning how to pimp the same way Uncle Sam, big business, and the power brokers in this world pimp. Learn how to pimp on that level, and at the same time, watch out for those who may want to pimp on you.

The real pimp game, the original pimp game that started this and every nation, will never change. PIMP— Put It in My Pocket! It's all about money and power, the control of dollars and people. The question you must answer for yourself is: Are you a pimp or a ho? I was born a pimp, and I will die a pimp.

PIMPTIONARY

A lot of these words and phrases have crossed over into everyday use, but they originated in the pimp game.

blade a street where hoes work (also *track*)

bottom bitch a pimp's main ho, the one who rides in the front seat

break yourself a command to a ho to give her pimp all of her money or choose another pimp

bumpin' taking another pimp's ho (also *knockin'*, *peelin'*)

burnout a ho who's been in it too long, is not on her game, and needs to get the hell out of the game

campaign the cars, jewels, minks, alligator shoes, and tailor-made clothes a pimp displays to get elected by the hoes

certified real, in reference to a real pimp or ho

choose when a ho selects a pimp and breaks herself

checkin' to verbally or physically put an out-of-pocket ho in her place

coming through a pimp door when a ho chooses a new pimp

cook to prepare a sucker to take his money

coonin' to knock a pimp by disregarding the rules and playing dirty

cop and blow to obtain and then lose, hopefully with some class

date a trick

double breasted when a pimp has double duties, such as also being a drug dealer or thief

down on ten toes totally in a pimp's corner, in reference to hoes

drop it like it's hot a pimp's command for a ho to break herself

fresh work a green ho

frosted flakes a sugar-coated, fake pimp, not the real deal

giving the blues harassing a ho to the point where it's difficult for her to work, sometimes for years at a time

green inexperienced in the game

head cut to beat a ho

hoboing fake ho'ing, playin' games (also *tippytoeing*)

ho drunk having the qualities of a burnout

ho up to choose a pimp

holding hands and kickin' cans trying to make a ho into a housewife

household a stable of three or more hoes

indoor pimp a pimp who works the escort services, clubs, or casinos

ism good, certified pimpin'

jug a favor or helping hand, usually done for a good pimp who fell off

long green big money, as opposed to "short" or small money

macaroni dressing flashy or someone who does, such as a ladies' man or pimp

mack a pimp, short for macaroni

mad move when a ho chooses a new pimp because she's temporarily mad at her old pimp, usually only to go back to him

mashin' for a ration a ho really getting that money for her pimp

mis-pimpin' misdirection from a simp

OD'd on the P burned out on ho'ing, prone to arguing, fussing, and fighting

OG original gangster; an old-school hustler

on blast crowded, in reference to a track

out of pocket when the ho does something wrong, like argue, look at another pimp, or try to run off another ho in her household

outdoor pimp a one-hundred-percent track pimp; outdoor pimps think they're better than indoor pimps

P a pimp

pimp arrest when a pimp forces a renegade to either break herself or get off the track

pimp pass when a pimp doesn't sweat another pimp's ho, out of respect or as a favor

peckerwood white ho (also *pink toe, snow bunny*)

playin' games when a ho isn't trying to choose a pimp and do some certified ho'ing

reckless eyeballin' when a ho looks at another pimp when he is sweating her, instead of holding her head down and crossing the street to get away from him (also *cross-eyed, googly-eyed*)

renegade a ho on the track, despite not having a pimp

roastin' the dozens in the street between two pimps

Scooby snack when a pimp fucks a ho and doesn't get any money; it's frowned upon

scratch money

senior citizen a ho older than twenty-four or a pimp in his thirties

serving a ho's new pimp notifying her old pimp of the change in situation

shake something to knock somebody else's ho

shit on talk bad about

simp fake pimp

solo bolo renegade

square someone who is a "regular" person, not a pimp

stable wrecker a ho who will argue, fight, and create strife in a household

stand-up real or certified, in reference to a pimp or ho

stroll old-school track

sucker a new pimp who can't get it right

sugar daddy a trick who pays a ho's bills, buys her things, and takes care of her, instead of just paying each time he has sex with her

sweating trying to persuade, convince, or harass a ho into leaving her old pimp

tender under the zipper a pimp who lets his little head beat out his big head

thoroughbred a good ho

tippytoeing hoboing

tools a pimp's campaign

track a blade

trap scratch a pimp gets from a ho

trick a customer or date

turnout a ho who is introduced to the game for the first time

weak dick tender under the zipper

whip a flashy car, part of a pimp's campaign

wife-in-law a fellow ho in a household

ACKNOWLEDGMENTS

I owe my thanks to the game and to the people who made it possible for me to put this together. First I'd like to thank Ferlisha Ivy and my five children: Takiyah Ivy, Kenneth Ajani Ivy Jr., Cala Reed, Kenneth Supreme Ivy Jr., Kendriona Ivy a.k.a. Ladybug, and my other kids, Javonte, Kenisha, and Kenyetta. My mother and father, Juanita and Collie Ivy (RIP), who gave me life. My brothers and sisters: Rosemary, Theresa, Collie, Tony (keep your head up, boy, in the joint), Marvin, Elijah, Lynette, and Evelyn. And to my cousins Reggie, Tywanda, Lester, Victor, Ricky, Danny, Al, Sheila, Zelma, and Nuke. To Linda, Regina, Tanya, and Mark, and all y'all down there in Oxford, Mississippi. Special thanks to Eduard Davis, Karen Hunter, and Jeremie Ruby-Strauss, who first came to me and said, Let's put this book out to the world. To the entire Simon & Schuster staff for their energetic and enthusiastic support and promoting this book in the same manner that Def Jam promotes records. To all the folks from Milwaukee who ever walked the Earth with me: JD a.k.a. Father Divine, Pimpin' Poke, Rob Roberson, Tommy Dixon, John Brown, Little Bear, Sonny Paige, Bobby Hill, Starchild, Sammy, Memphis a.k.a. Tick Tock, BJ, Petey Paige, Brandy (RIP), Flip a.k.a. June Bug (RIP), Marty Freeman, Grit, K-Mack, Little Daddy, CC, Twan, Mr. Terry, Pimp Little, Mick, John Carter, Pimpin' Paul, Hollywood, King Gus, Pimp Ike, Old Man Pimpin' Ike (RIP), Lefty, Kemp, Kurt Blow, Ronny Jewel, Slim, Elroy (RIP), Pimpin' Snooky, Pimpin' T-Bone, Greg Farmer, Little Rob, Pimpin' Sam, Pimpin' Scoob, the Great Poke, Funtaine, Johnny Goodlow (RIP), Triple D, Superb, Twonyae (RIP),

Dorele, Sluggo, Big B, Mark Wave, Chicago, Gene, Willie D, Kickin' It Jack, Thomas, Old Man Running Bear, Milwaukee Buck, my cousin Greasy, Sackson, Mack the Knife, Julius Nash, Kool in Dickie, Sonny Carter, Baby Love, Chris Soloman, Memphis Jake, Esquire, Billy Bugs, Melvin Grant and the Grant family, Ted Beamon, Mike Beamon, Ray Lynn, Dae Dae, Priest, Karl Sloan and the Sloan family, Pimpin' Stand, Chris Taylor, Walbash, Sport, CB, Boo Boo, Brian Ivory, Leroy Bell, E-Noble, Frankie Fox, Jay Fox, Sport (AC), J Rock, Young CB, Danny Tubs, Michael Tubs, and for all my other friends out of Milwaukee that I didn't mention—I have not forgotten y'all! I would also like to acknowledge a few players from Milwaukee: Frog, Elliot, Poppa Quin, Eastside Quawn, Jim Dandy, Pee Wee Ferguson, Brian Ferguson, John Ferguson and the Ferguson family, Seahorse, Reggie, my brother from another mother Porter Magee, Big K, Buzzer James, Don, Mike Banks, Greg Bradford, Greg Groves, Little Greg, C Money, Leonard Ross, the Eastside homies, KG, Tree, Chris Davis (RIP), Doo Doo, Jay Rowe, Baby Drew, Big Kurt, Marvell, Little June (RIP), Elliot (RIP), Mario (RIP), Earl the Pearl, La La, Parish, L.A., Corey, Baby Dad, Big Tone, Bohannon, Twan, Dawan, Stacy, Bruce, Mick, Rob, Little Corey (on the beats), Short Mack, Camaci, Porgi, Smoke, Charlie Mack, Perry, Toot, The Twins, Black D, Action Blue, Oily Mike, Michelle, JD (RIP), Scottie a.k.a. SB. To my Puerto Rican friends: Sam, Harvey, Richie, and Angel. To some more of my player friends: Cash Ball, Young Twan, Young'un, Craig and Tom from Club Escape, Deven from Club Questions, Yancy (the valet man), CooCoo Cal, Ralph, Smalls, Smitty Darbie, Steve Snowball, 2-4 Tweet (RIP), 2-4 RC (RIP), Germ, Pig, Precious, Arby, Money Mike, Reesco, Teddy a.k.a. Tim. To my nieces and nephews: Jessie, Sherise, Chris, Andrenna, Taurus, Renee, Dominique,

Lamontre, Kentwan, Zaresha, Marajsha, Antroness, Cortez, Anisha, Tekeda, Lakeya, Tyquesha, Shatorya. To all my international friends: T Banks, Pimpsy, Ivory P, Suave, Young Rick, Governor, Napoleon, Skinny, Daytona D, Valentino, JuJu, King Burt, King James, Brink, King Boo (RIP), Good Game, Reverend Seamore, Bishop Don Magic Juan, Scooter G, Ronny Slim, Avalanche, Candy, Little Candy, Love, GA (Game Affiliated), Be Rich, Jap, Mackie, Bobby, RP, Kansas City's Finest, Gorgeous Dre, Wichita Playa Fats, Fast, Gangsta Brown, Fillmore Slim, DC Buttons, Bubblicious, Pimp CC from California, Antwan, Mr. Bolden, Big Silk, Spectacular, Shorty P, Ross from Cleveland, Godfather, Cash from ATL, Revenue, Charm, Reverend Toby, Vic Mighty Brown, Brick from the West Side of Chicago, Mike Maroy from Too Real for TV, Burroughs, Scorpio, King Bean (RIP), Slick Vic, Chick Boss, John Dough, Atlantic Red, Don Fetti, Little D, J Mitch, Isreal, D from Nashville, Tim and Terrell from Nashville, Lex from ATL, Cool Ace, Sheep Dog, Will, Alex from Mississippi, Bobby Brome, Pocket Knife (RIP), Dooby from LA, Segel, Linch-Bay, Dr. William Bay, Cornell, Christ, Goldie McDowell, T from Nashville, California Mike, Succeed, Memphis Black, Success, Rico from Memphis, White Folks, Blue Diamond, Supreme, Smiley, International Red, Mack Slim, Little Ronny Slim, Mr. Tate, Payday, Mack Dre. To all my friends in hip-hop who helped me come up: Pimp C, Bun B, Too $hort, Juvenile, J Reezy from Detroit Cartel, 50 Cent, Mack 10, Pastor Troy, Project Pat, Lil Jon, Trillville, Lil Scrappy, Slim Thug, Mike Jones, Young Jeezy, T.I. and the Pimp Squad Clique (Big Country, Young Dro, C Rod), Chamillionaire, Jermaine Dupri, Nelly, P Diddy, Loon, Reality from FUP Mob, Paper Chase, Stackin Cheese, David Banner, Lil' Flip, Red Eyes, Baby and Lil Wayne from Cash Money Records, Young Boss, OutKast,

Snoop Dogg, U Dig Records, Fabolous, Raekwon, Nick Cannon, Fat Man Scoop, Ed Lover, K Slay, Young Buck, Greg Street, Frank Ski, *Source* magazine, *F.E.D.S.* magazine, *Vibe* magazine, *XXL* magazine, *Ozone Magazine*, Cheddar DVD, *Street Magazine*, Scarface, Jay Prints, Young Bleed, Yukmouth, Comedian Shorty, Comedian Davole, Da Brat, Gangster Boo, Boo and Gottie, 112, Jagged Edge, Usher, E-40, Skip and Waco from UTP, Biz Markie, Bow Wow, Ice-T, Lloyd Banks, C-Bone, Skim, Steve Harvey, Cedric the Entertainer, Big Mike, Gip, Ali, C-Lo, C-Bo (Goodie Mob), Show Time, Third, Decatur Black, Player Puncho, Rico Love, DJ Funky, Tony Neal, Homer Blow, DJ Don, Reggie Brown, Core DJs, Kid Capri, Mike Pratt, DJ Dimp, Mommy True La, Jazzy Pha, Nitty, Shorty Red, Faybo, Dem Franchise Boys, Ying Yang Twins, 8-Ball, MJG, Magic from Magic City, Casper, Stainless Entertainment, Young City Chopper, T-Gray, Archie Lee, Eddie Kane, E from the Outsiders, J Prince, Track Boys, St. Lunatics, Keywan, Murphy Lee, Danny Christian, Benny Boon, David Palmer, Chris Robertson, Chingy, DeShay Jones from D Productions, Lil Boosie and Lil Webby, Dub C, Dru Down, C Note, The Game, Nas, Jadakiss, Whodini, and many, many more. Last thanks to Latasha Finch, Dopeman from ChronicCentral.Net, Terrel from Morgan Designs, C-Money from No Nonsense, Marvin Ivy from Ivy-Media, Jayrol from Eye to Eye Records, Steve-O from Infinite Records, Debbie the Glass Lady, Al Allston, Terrel from Shoot 2 Films, Jay Dog from Selective Hits Distribution, Tiffany Flowers, Carla from Dallas, Black the Vet Ho from Dallas, Donald Jet, B-Dog, Avie the Pimp, Ed from Nashville, Lil Farrakan from Milwaukee, Chug, Pokie, Poonie, Ren, Big Meech from BMF, Fiskani, and George Karem out of Atlanta.